POST MOVES:

The Female Athlete's Guide to Dominate Life After College

By ANGELA LEWIS

Published in the United States by Global Athlete Media Network.

St. Louis, MO

ISBN-10: 0-9981339-0-6

ISBN-13: 978-0-9981339-0-4

Additional Publications by Angela Lewis:

The Game Changing Assist: Six Simple Ways to Choose Success

The Game Changing Assist: Six Simple Ways to Choose Success Workbook

To order books in bulk contact Global Athlete Media Network at info@globalathletemedia.com.

Table of Contents

ACKNOWLEDGEMENTS

The women in this book are forever grateful to the people who supported our athletic goals. We understand that it is now our responsibility to provide these same opportunities for other young women. As a result, a portion of the proceeds from *Post Moves* will be donated to the Women's Sports Foundation (WSF). Given WSF's long standing history, global impact on young women and research on girls participation in sports, we are honored to support the Women's Sports Foundation.

The Women's Sports Foundation, founded in 1974 by tennis icon and civil rights pioneer Billie Jean King, is dedicated to creating leaders by ensuring girls' access to sports. The Foundations provides safe and equitable sports opportunities so that all girls receive the significant health, education and leadership benefits both on and off the field. One of the top five public grant-giving women's funds in the United States, the Foundation distributes upwards of $10,000 per week from operating dollars to provide opportunities for socioeconomically underprivileged and inactive girls to participate in sports and physical activity.

Over the past 41 years, the Foundation has awarded more than $50 million in programming to advance participation, research and leadership in sports and physical activity for girls and women. WSF major grant programs range from getting over 1 million girls active in physical activity (GoGirlGo); to providing grass-roots sports opportunities to over 6,000 girls of color aged 11-18 (Sports 4 Life); and over 1,300 grants to aspiring champion athletes and teams to help defray the expensive travel, training and equipment expenses required for them to reach their championship potential (Travel & Training Fund).

Over the past 30 years, the Foundation has produced more than 40 national, evidence-based research studies that provide a data driven approach to gender equity. Research informs our advocacy and forms the basis of how the organization develops its programs. WSF continues to advocate for Title IX of the Education Amendments of 1972 by working with the NCAA leadership, the Office of Civil Rights, coaching organizations, parents and the media to provide education and guidance to achieve compliance of the law. Title IX protects people from the discrimination based on sex in education programs or activities that receive Federal financial assistance.

The Foundation's Athlete Leadership Connection initiative underscores the WSF's commitment to supporting champion female athletes in two major ways. First, by providing the resources, education and network they need to become powerful leaders while competing and secondly, acting as the conduit through which champion athletes can make a successful transition from their playing careers to their next professional challenge. For more information visit www.womenssportsfoundation.org.

INTRODUCTION

Playing sports has provided tremendous opportunities for me to visit places I never thought I could go and meet people that would have a lasting positive impact on my life. For these two reasons alone, I am thankful that I was able to play basketball throughout my youth, in college and professionally.

It is widely documented that participating can have a tremendous impact on the lives of young women. Studies have shown an increased level of confidence, body satisfaction and leadership ability with girls. All of these findings are true for my life and the fifteen contributors to *Post Moves: The Female Athlete's Guide to Dominate Life After College*.

This book is written for female college athletes by former college and professional athletes who have transitioned to successful careers. After I finished playing basketball overseas, I coached college basketball and realized that the young women I coached had the same struggles I faced at their age. Ever since I stopped coaching, it has been on my heart to write this book for female college athletes and introduce them to other women whose experiences will help them recognize the options that exist beyond playing sports.

Most college students face difficulty determining their next steps because life after college is definitely a significant transition. Nevertheless, this transition is often magnified when you are an athlete. Student-athletes' coaches, athletic administrators, and academic advisors orchestrate most of their time which creates a consistent routine. Once that routine isn't in place, many athletes are lost without coaches to help guide or professional mentors to offer advice.

There's a myriad of reasons why athletes leave school unprepared and given the disparities in compensation between women and men, this book is of even more importance. Women earn less money than men in the workplace, but having a strong set of mentors to guide you through the process can mitigate some of the challenges with finding a fulfilling career.

As a result, each chapter gives the contributor's current occupation, lists her thoughts in question and answer format and ends with her contact information. This book was intentionally designed to allow the reader to get the answers to questions quickly and to have immediate access to fifteen dynamic women who are all willing to answer questions and provide guidance.

You will find each contributor has a unique background and shares her experiences authentically. Some of the themes from this book are 1) there is not a straight line to accomplishing any goal, 2) try even though you are scared and 3) entrepreneurship is a viable option for female athletes.

There are situations that will occur in life that don't go as planned and how you respond makes the difference. For example, Peppi Browne-Armstrong played basketball at Duke University and was drafted to the WNBA's Charlotte Sting after her senior year in college. However, she already signed a contract for a job after graduation. She was able to negotiate the terms of the contract to make sure she would start that role once the WNBA's season ended. Also, Peppi looked to make strategic moves in her career she returned to school full time, having to drive over two hours each day to earn an MBA while she had children and was married. These unexpected changes occur often.

Pasha Cook dropped out of high school once she became academically ineligible her junior year. She was able to bounce back and receive a scholarship at the age of 24. Pasha finished her collegiate playing career at the University of Memphis and is now an empowerment speaker and author. Her multiple failed plans required courage.

Each of contributors experienced multiple failures along the way but continued to persist despite disappointments and being afraid at times. Courage is not the absence of fear. Instead, courage is moving forward in the face of fear, which the contributors of this book demonstrated. Each woman told the story about a time when they felt they weren't prepared, but they made a decision that intentionally to be uncomfortable in order to grow professionally.

Lisa Mecili-Standage played basketball at Truman State University and worked at a fitness club immediately after graduating. She was quickly recognized as a leader and offered a position in California at 24 years old. Although she faced many challenges in that role, being willing to go taught her what it takes to be a leader. Those early lessons laid the foundation for her future success because she now owns her own company.

Priscilla Pacheco Tallman was a standout volleyball player at the University of Georgia who decided to use a temp agency to help her find work after graduation. After giving birth to her son, she suffered from postpartum depression and had the courage to ask for help. Having been a successful athlete, it was challenging for her to let people know that she needed additional support, but it was a pivotal moment in her life. She now inspires people through her writing and coaching volleyball.

The third theme that you read was an unexpected surprise that thirteen of the fifteen contributors are entrepreneurs. Some of the women work full time while running their business while other women have larger businesses. Nevertheless, each woman agreed that playing sports prepared them for the entrepreneurial journey.

Erica Smith played college basketball at Southern Illinois University at Carbondale but always had a love for sports and business. As a college student, she helped started a few businesses and worked in leadership capacities for a few different companies. After her mother became ill, she decided to pursue that entrepreneurial path and is now the co-owner of a youth basketball club called Machine Elite. She uses the teamwork skills she learned as a collegiate athlete to help players develop on and off the court. Erica is also the founder of Second Wind which focuses on helping college athletes transition better to life after college.

Similarly, with a love for sports business and community, Khalia Collier is the owner and General Manager of the St. Louis Surge, a professional women's basketball team. Khalia played basketball at Columbia College but after multiple injuries, transferred to Missouri Baptist on a golf scholarship. She strategically selected jobs while in college that provided business training and became the owner of the Surge at 24 years old. Now in the fifth year, the team has won two WBCBL National Championships and boasts nearly 3,000 fans each home game with the players serving as role models to young girls in the region.

With a heart for service and educational equity, Alicia Herald is the founder of MyEdMatch, a technology company that pairs prospective teachers with schools that are a good fit. Alicia played basketball for the championships winning Washington University in St. Louis. After undergrad, she became a teacher through Teach for America and moved to Los Angeles to teach, and subsequently opened a Teach for American office in Kansas City. Alicia recognized the turnover rate in education was extremely high in schools with the greatest needs so she decided to create a solution to the problem. Alicia utilizes the leadership skills learned from playing sports to create change in the lives of youth and educators.

These examples are a short preview of what's to come. As you know, anything you strive for with passion and persistence will require work. Your test along the way will determine how committed you are to what you said you want.

Female athletes are equipped with everything they need to create the life they desire. The drive, determination, and ability to work in a team are invaluable traits. Over the course of the fifteen chapters, you will learn the often unspoken rules of achieving success after playing sports. Remember to enjoy the journey and use what you've learned to help others along the way.

Chapter 1: PEPPI BROWNE-ARMSTRONG

Current occupation: Executive Briefing Consultant at IBM and Founder of Docentz.

Where did you attend college and what sport did you play?

Peppi Browne-Armstrong: I played basketball at Duke University.

What was your major?

Peppi Browne-Armstrong: Undergrad at Duke. I majored in biological anthropology and anatomy, electrical engineering and biomedical engineering. After that, I went to grad school at UNC and got a master's degree in biomedical engineering and minor in business as well. Then went to Wake Forest and got my MBA.

What factors impacted your decision to go down this particular career path?

Peppi Browne-Armstrong: I went to a magnet high school and the projects that I did in high school fostered what I felt like I wanted to do in college. When I got to Duke, I wasn't in the school of engineering. I actually applied to get in after my sophomore year, but

I started off with biology because I always just wanted to do something with anatomy. We had additional credits that we could do in high school. I thought that was great so I just wanted to continue that in college. That's what led me down that path initially. Then engineering because, "Hey, who loves to tinker with stuff? Me." I was able to blend both together.

I was lucky in high school. I took a lot of AP courses. My freshman year went pretty smoothly. My academic transition to get from high school to college was pretty smooth. I was able to take a lighter load when I got to college.

How did you prepare to leave college? What was your first job? How did you secure your first job?

Peppi Browne-Armstrong: My first job was with Eli Lilly and Company, a large pharmaceutical company here in the States. This is not just something that I did my senior year. Let me start by saying that. I went to as many of the job fairs that I could when I didn't have practice. I missed several of them because I didn't even know they were around. Then I started literally asking all of my non-athletic friends, "Hey, what's going on?" That type of thing kept me informed.

After a while, they would say, "So and so is coming here," or there were some interview sessions. At these sessions the hiring manager, maybe a couple of others from some of the local companies would come and have a session in a classroom to give us information about the company.

I went to info sessions and they also came to the job fairs. Every year, Eli Lilly had a branch that was local to the Durham area and every year, Eli Lilly had a booth at the career fair. Every year, I was at that booth and I got to know the hiring manager. I would say, "How are you doing?" The first couple of times it was more like just shooting the breeze, "What do you guys have available?"

I did my research at the beginning. I knew they were a pharmaceutical company. I knew several other things, but for the most part, when I went to those job fairs, I was trying to get to know the people so they would recognize me when my resume came over, "Oh yeah, I met this girl. She did blah, blah, blah. We talked. She's really cool." That type of thing. The first couple of times, that was really the cool.

Then by the time junior or senior year, you're like, "Yeah, I'm ready for the job part. Don't forget about me. Remember me, the one with the smiling face." That type of thing. I did the same thing with info sessions. It was the same people. Remember that. It's the same people that go to the info sessions that are at these job fairs. Same people. Get to know them especially if you're really doing your research and talking to that company. That's pretty much what I did.

It sounds like you had a strategy in place. What was your game plan?

Peppi Browne-Armstrong: I will say I have a plan A, plan B, plan C and a plan D. I already had a plan D because there're some things I can control and there're some things I just can't control. I couldn't control tearing my ACL, but I had plan B, and if that didn't work out, plan C, plan D. It was a game plan. No doubt about it!

What was your thought process with wanting to work at Eli Lilly? Why did you pick that company?

Peppi Browne-Armstrong: One was location. I did pick about five locations where I would want to live. A lot of that had to do with places where I was comfortable living. I looked at the cost of living. I looked at where my family was. I love to travel. I still love to travel. I was looking at access in and out. If I have to go real quick to DC, Florida or Atlanta I wanted to be able to do that. There were a couple of places where I was like, "I know the market." I had an idea of the job market. Had an idea of the housing market. You've definitely had to look at benefits. Hands down, you've got to look at those benefits. Don't forget those benefits. Very important.

What are some benefits that transitioning athletes should consider?

Peppi Browne-Armstrong: This is another interesting topic I talk about because people always think benefits are health benefits and how much you're getting paid. Yes, that is important, but there are other benefits that people overlook, that they can use in the negotiating process when they are at that final stage being hired. Other questions you should ask are: "Am I going to get company stock after a certain number of years or months even when I'm there?" "What's the vacation policy?" Vacation is very important. Everybody needs to make sure they get out, but most people don't know, you get the average two weeks. A lot of times you're not allowed to take any days until after you work five months. Sometimes you can negotiate that right away because you never know what's going to happen.

Those are the two things that have come up as the forefront and they were for me, but don't forget about those working from home. "Can I work from home two to three times a week? Is that all right?" Flexible working hours are a consideration. Some people work for four days and are off for two. There's a lot of things that are negotiable so I will also tell people: "Don't forget about those intangibles when you're looking for a job."

What has been your career progression since your first job?

Peppi Browne-Armstrong: I wanted to both do programming and science. My first job was an automation engineer. Basically, I was in the lab running the experiments in the lab to do the drug testing. This was very, very early stage drug testing. It was a really, really tiny amount of liquid, and I had to actually have to program the machine to do what I wanted it to do. For example, the machine had to move 10 milliliters from here to over there, but it was like 365 of them that had to be programmed to move at the same time. From there, I had to check to make sure it worked and functioned properly. That's pretty much what I did in my first job. I liked it.

What was your career progression from there?

Peppi Browne-Armstrong: In my second job, I felt like I wanted to be a little bit more towards the customer. When you're very at the early stage in pharmaceuticals, you don't know if this particular drug, or whole sets of drugs you're working on, is even going to make it up to the end goal. Therefore, I started to wonder what that end result would be. My next job was, I approached it from the standpoint of "Let me see if I can get in front of the customer, more in front of the client from there." At the same time, that's when I started my graduate work as well so I was getting some patient interaction as well.

It just so happened that Medicare part D came along from new legislation. Then all of a sudden, they were like, "Can anybody program that knows how to do related to anything medical?" They were just hiring. I was like, "Yeah, I can do programming. I definitely know medical stuff and jargon. I can do that." I worked for the federal government on Medicare part D, which was very eye opening. In that role, I was working directly with the person who was trying to apply, couldn't understand it. It was a fun job and very interesting.

From there, I learned, that was a bit too much interaction with the customer for me, so I pulled back. I decided to get an MBA because I knew I wanted to do more of the business side. I wanted to see the end result, but I also wanted to be able to use my brain and be more creative. Not that I wasn't using my brain before, but somebody was telling me directly what to do in my second job, "You've got to do this, this, that or that. Just do it. I don't care how you do it. Just do it."

I felt if I got my MBA, I'd be able to say, "Here's the problem overall. Let's see how I can solve it." It was a little bit more of a strategy type job or position I was going for again, using all the other skills that I acquired beforehand.

When I left the MBA, I went to IBM and decided on marketing because I thought marketing was cool. I could do drawing, design and use more of the creative side of my brain as well. For example, the fact that people walk into the store and they go to the right because we drive on the right-hand side. It's stuff a little like that that I found interesting. There's little subtle things that I learned while getting my MBA that I think have led me to this current position where I'm at now.

It's really interesting to know you saw that you wanted to learn something new and then you made a decision to continue your education beyond undergrad. How did you know which additional degrees to pursue?

Peppi Browne-Armstrong: The short answer is I didn't know. I had to ask. Back in the day, the companies would pay for you to go get your degree or to go to school. By the way, this is another intangible that you need to make sure that you can try and get in from an employer if you can. I was like, "Look, you're going to pay for me. Hey, let's see, what's my options? Let's see what I could do, whatever," but I still have to like it because it's going to be grueling, the same double schedule that you had in undergrad.

Instead of going from practice to class, you're going from work to class. It's the same juggling, so it's not going to be easy. That's what prompted me to go to school the first time. Then, I looked at all these different options. Obviously, I went and interviewed at different schools and saw what they had.

The decision to go back to business school was different because I had to pay. I thought, "If I have to pay, I've got to really make sure I know what I'm doing because I'm not getting this money back." In this situation as well, I went to more info sessions related to getting my MBA than anything else just because I knew just the price tag of the MBA. You want to make sure that you get the best school possible for you.

There's a lot more that went into it at least for me than going to grad school the first time. I hate to say it. It seems like a broken record, but as with everything, you have to just ask and prepare. My motto is: No question is a dumb question. Even in class, I will be that one that if I don't understand, I'm asking you 10 zillion times, "Why do you put that there?" I'm raising my hand. That's just me. That's how I operate.

I will say I use LinkedIn ... I think probably because it wasn't really as big when I went to school for basketball first time, but during my MBA, I was on LinkedIn. I went to large, national-wide job fairs.

Flew all the way to California, Atlanta, and even St. Louis. Anything that I could sign up for within that 2-year period, I did it.

What challenges did you have with your different career choices?

Peppi Browne-Armstrong: One challenge was showing people my resume and they saw all the biotech or health care yet I wanted to do marketing. Some people wouldn't even look at my resume. They were like, "Why? What do you have to bring to the table?" I struggled with my resume a lot, especially the second go round to get a job. I think also that's why I went to get my MBA even though I was one of the older students there.

What ways do you de-stress from your work environment?

Peppi Browne-Armstrong: One way is I try not to stress at all. At the end of the day, me getting a heart attack is not worth this job. I'm going to try not to stress. That's just my rule.

I tend to do creative projects. I'm usually doing something that is total opposite maybe of what I was doing at work or doing at school. If I'm doing science all day, I'm doing nothing related to science when I'm off work. Forget it.

I guess at the end of the day too, you find what you love. If you're lucky enough, you're doing a job that you really, really love. If you're not that lucky, then make sure you do take time out to do what you love and block it off on your calendar. I started to do that now and it's made a whole lot of difference because you get refreshed when you come back and you go, "All right. Time to go to work."

What are some examples of the ways you've used what you've learned from sports in your day-to-day work life?

Peppi Browne-Armstrong: From a team sport aspect, I do think having to work with different personalities is something you learn how to do from being on a team. Having already been exposed to working with people with different personalities definitely does help.

There're things that you do not get back: time, money and energy. You have to manage those 3. I was taught that from very early. It's ingrained in the brain—time, money and energy. If something is going to take a good chunk of my time, good chunk of my money, good chunk of my energy, I'd better know how to manage it properly.

I think sports also teaches you how to manage your time. Even in high school, you've got to go to class, then you've got to go to your practice right after. In college, same thing except you might have training table on top of that and a couple of other things. The rules don't change. It's just what pulls at your time over the years but it's the same type of mentality I think just from high school all the way through. Just to be prepared.

Yeah, what's your thought process when creating a plan?

Peppi Browne-Armstrong: First again, you have to know the end goal. Yeah, that's the first thing. If you don't know where you're going, then you can't plan for it. Most of the time, the other things that are involved are usually related to money, usually related to time. You have to consider how much time it is going to be pulling on you and what will you have to stop doing to make it happen. Then lastly, it's usually a regional question. The reason I say that is people have to live somewhere. They got to be able to afford it. There's a reason why there is a teacher shortage in Hawaii. Nobody can afford to live there, but that's something you have to take into account when you're getting a job.

When you get kids, you got to have people around that could help you. It takes a village. It does take a village. Don't let anybody tell you differently. Number 2. Money is tight for everybody and expenses just happen. You don't even know. There's a lot you have to take into account and most of it is related to time and money and then where you want to live.

If you start your planning that way, you're pretty much okay.

What should you do if following your passion doesn't allow you to live comfortably?

Peppi Browne-Armstrong: If you're lucky, you can follow your passion. I chose to follow my passion on somebody else's dime because I knew I had to live. I got to eat. I have to live somewhere, but if you start your passion or if it's not readily available to you, that doesn't mean you should give up on your passion.

Basically, all I'm saying is just do it; start it on the side. Start it on the side. Start your own business. Start making those connections. Start doing that on the side on somebody else's dime. Still get that paycheck. Still get those benefits. You work from home sometimes? Block off two hours so you could do your passion on the side.

Knowing that, that was what I decided to do. It's not for everybody, but if you think about it in another way, you were already doing it in college. You were getting your education on somebody else's dime. Don't say you weren't working hard for it. You were definitely working hard for it, but that's what you were doing. You were doing your passion on somebody else's dime.

What are the final pieces of advice you would like to share with current female student-athletes?

Peppi Browne-Armstrong: What makes this transition any different once you get out into the workforce and the real world? You already were doing it. You have the backbone. You have the skill. You have the knowledge. You were already doing it so just continue. It's just a different thing to manage. Instead of juggling a basketball, a book, and food or, you're juggling some finance deal. Take the basketball out, you're juggling money on top of it something like that. You were already doing it.

Peppi Browne-Armstrong's Contact Information:
Email: confessionsofasa@gmail.com
Website: www.docentz.com

Chapter 2: KHALIA COLLIER

Current occupation: Owner and General Manager of the St. Louis Surge.

Where did you attend college and what sport did you play?

Khalia Collier: Right out of high school, I was a Division I recruit. I was looking at colleges all over. It was interesting to me because I had a big head coming out of high school. I wanted to go to this big DI school. I ended up finding a small school right next door to Mizzou, Columbia College, that I felt like was going to be the perfect school for me. It's NAIA Division I, extremely competitive, but I didn't have the best experience there. I ended up leaving after two years. I learned some hard lessons in a short period of time. I grew up pretty fast.

Having the opportunity to come back home to St. Louis and attended Missouri Baptist University to be closer to my family. I was super injury prone and didn't have the college career I expected at all. Luckily for me, I played golf in high school.

Not many people are able to go from a full-ride basketball scholarship to a full-ride golf scholarship. This was a huge opportunity for me, but I never stopped missing the game of basketball. It was a part of my blood because I had been playing since I was five. I knew that, somehow, I would always be around sports. I just didn't know what capacity.

What did you major in? Then, what did you do immediately when you finished?

Khalia Collier: I majored in Communications and Political Science. It was interesting because in my senior year of college, I actually worked in corporate. I worked for Plaza Motors at the time. I was working about 40 to 50 hours a week. I was also prepping for the LSAT because after college, I was going to law school.

Instead, this opportunity came available, to be a part of corporate, in the automotive industry, and to join their management team. I was the youngest and the only female. I felt like this is a perfect opportunity for me to join a Fortune 500 company and take on a strong leadership role. That's exactly what I did. I just love work. I figured I would get some experience in my resume early on and law school could still be there if I decided to go back. I started working 70 hours a week. I was really, really good at what I did. Finance and sales is my background. But I really missed being around sports, and I could never shake that feeling.

Why did you start working for Plaza when you were a senior in college? How did that come about?

Khalia Collier: It's weird. I didn't have your typical childhood. I've always worked, strangely enough, probably from the fifth grade through middle school I worked at a flea market. I worked every weekend. I sold car products, and I'd go from car wash to car wash selling car products. I had the opportunity to make some really good money while in school; it was just like, "Why wouldn't I?" Golf wasn't as strenuous as basketball, so I had some flexibility in my schedule.

But, I think the opportunity came about because I was really getting to know people and building relationships early on. I was a huge proponent of meeting as many people as I could and just networking. It paid off for me at a really early age.

How did you get the job at Plaza? How do you make decisions about where you are going to get a position?

Khalia Collier: I will say that job came from who I knew. I knew someone who was working there. They were able to vouch for me. I'd already worked really hard. A big part of life is positioning yourself to be successful. It's not just a situation where you know somebody and they pull you in. Instead, you have to already be on top of your stuff, and by the way, you know somebody. Then they will pull me in. That's exactly how I got the job.

They knew I was looking for it and I was working for another company before. I was in marketing. They were like, "Hey, you could probably be pretty good at this." I'm a car buff, so it made sense. I'm big on do what you're already naturally good at. I was naturally good at it, so I went for it.

People underestimate their warm market all the time. You have a warm market that's always around you. It's just identifying what you want to do.

Your warm market is your immediate network—your friends, your family, their friends, their family—that is just one degree of separation from you.

It's super key for you to know who's in your circle, whether that's attorneys, whether that's doctors, accountants. If you start to develop what you're interested in early, you get to know those people a little bit better. You ask them, can you volunteer. Can you job shadow? You get exposed to as much as you can. That's what I did at an early age. I was exposed to just about everything because I put myself in positions to be exposed to it.

I wanted to know what I didn't want to do more than what I wanted to do. What better way to start than your own warm market of figuring out who can help you volunteer, internships or get a job?

How important is it to have people in your corner willing to help you accomplish your goals?

Khalia Collier: Self-made doesn't exist. No matter who you are, someone helped you get there. It's really important, when asking someone to put their name on the line for you, that you're 110% ready for that opportunity as well.

Because you can't do stuff like that prematurely. Unfortunately, if you vouch for the wrong person, it burns your credibility. I've seen that growing up. You've got to come ready. If I'm going to ask you to take that leap of faith on me, I want to give you every reason why you should do it.

How did you get connected with the Surge, which you ultimately owned?

Khalia Collier: It was actually really crazy how the Surge came into existence for me. The Surge was already here in St. Louis. They were playing at Vashon High School. They played at Flow Valley for a little while. They were averaging 50 to 60 people a game. They started back in 2008. I found out about the team from one of my good friends at SLU.

She was looking at trying out for the team. I had heard a little bit about the Surge, but it was probably something I would've never been interested in if she wouldn't have wanted to explore the opportunity to try out for the team. I went with her just to support a friend, to see what it was. We traveled out to East St. Louis. I was like, "Huh. This is interesting." I stayed, and just kind of got roped in.

When you don't have too many opportunities outside of playing overseas, you jump, as an athlete, at an opportunity to continue playing in your home city. That's exactly what a lot of the women were doing, who were playing for the Surge. I got roped into being the team manager. At the time, I was already working really crazy hours at work, but it gave me an opportunity to be around the game.

It literally went as fast as a month's transition for me. I went on to support a friend. Then after that, I became the team manager. Then, they asked me to play in one game with the Surge. I jumped in a couple of practices. I still kid all the time and say, "I still have some game, and if I wanted to, I could play." But I do know the truth deep down.

After I played a couple of games with the Surge, actually one game, a light bulb went off for me. I could take this, grow it into something really unique in the St. Louis market.

My goal was, at the time, to take over at the end of the season. I didn't think I was nearly ready. Wasn't talking about doing it now. But little did I know, he opted it to me to take it over the next week. So, I did.

I don't think I really even thought about it in my head. I didn't start thinking about it until I realized what I'd done. I was all, "God, I bought a basketball team. I should probably get a staff." Luckily for me, I've been blessed to have some of the most supportive friends and family in my life that stepped up, that help me grow it really early on.

In the beginning, with the Surge, I had no idea what I was getting myself into. What I did know was that I was going to do it to the best of my ability and that I was going to work as hard as I possibly could to create something different in the St. Louis market. Five years later, we are still growing and building today.

Talk about the progression of the Surge over the course of the five years. Because it has been a process. People are going to look at the Surge now and talk about what it is and not know the sacrifice that you've made for it to get here, personally and professionally.

Khalia Collier: It's interesting because I don't think people will ever understand the sacrifices, the hard work, the sleepless nights that's gone into building the team. Some of that is not for them to know, either. The progression has been dog years for me.

The past five years have been actual dog years. I've had so many hard lessons, so many life lessons. I've grown up in a very short period of time, becoming the business woman that I am today. Being able to have those experiences, the good with the bad, to really mold me into knowing my true vision of what I wanted the program to look like. I've had a lot of people help me along the way. They've really helped me perfect what the Surge is, not only as it is now, but what it's going to be in the next five to ten years.

Our first year, again, I had no idea what I was getting myself into. First year, people in the market are just surprised to see that you're around. Women's basketball has been untapped in St. Louis. People already have some negative connotations and some stereotypes that come along with it. By the second year, people were just surprised to see that we came back in 2013. In 2012, I'd gone through a lot of players, really figuring out the direction we wanted to head, as well as coaches, as well as the brand. We rebranded in 2013. We restructured the program to have the right product. That's what 2013 was. We were headed in that direction.

In 2014, you got to be a part of the magic of year three credibility. That's when I felt like, year three, I really understood what we were building for the long haul. The caliber of people that we wanted as a part of our program and why the Surge was so important for a community aspect.

We were putting, not just great basketball players on the court but great people together. That's when the philosophy of Bigger Than Basketball really started to grow. I knew that it was always going to be something bigger than the game, but now to see that the brand is what's so important to me. When you see Surge basketball, you know you're going to get the best talent and the greatest people that we can assemble possible. That's what makes people excited to watch.

That's what we shifted in 2015. We fell short in The National Championship, but I will forever say championships are the bonus. They're the cherry on top for us. We don't exist to win. We exist to build a community product, and then, by the way, we win. That's kind of how it goes.

This year is all about the 5th anniversary. Everyone knows, in business, to make it in five years as a startup, that's a milestone within itself. I'm proud to say that we're a women's franchise. We're not a non-profit. We're not a cause. We are a franchise that's building, that's growing. We've been able to get the endorsements of the St. Louis Blues. We have the Cardinals, now, supporting us. We're at a whole new level.

Khalia, I have so much respect and admiration for the work that you've done. I know there were nights when you slept at the office or you were eating egg sandwiches. You had a $50 per month food budget. How and when you made the decision to leave Plaza?

Khalia Collier: When I made the decision to leave Plaza, it was a very calculated move for me. I had been thinking about it for a while. I had to have some savings, so I planned for it. As much as it was a leap of faith, I'm a conservative risk-taker. You plan and then you take the risk. I wanted to know a little bit about what I was getting myself into financially. When I actually made the decision to leave my full-time position, I heard nothing but, "That's a horrible idea. You're making the worst mistake of your life. At what age are you going to be making this money doing this?" But I didn't want to do Surge for money. I feel like when you do what you love, money will come. I felt like this was the right opportunity for me to go for it.

In 2012, I will never forget the date because it was Valentine's Day, February 14th, I left my job and I went full-time Surge. It was one of the best decisions I could've ever made. To take the time, the heart, the dedication, and to pour it all in. Failure was not an option for me.

I can honestly tell you, it just wasn't an option. The worst-case scenario for me was I was going to get another job. If that was my worst-case, I was going to be okay. I had some cushion in the bank. I had some ride or die family who were going to let me sleep on their couch. I drove a really nice car right out of college. I figured, if I'm sleeping in the back of my Lexus, I could have worse problems, so I'll be all right.

Many people decide to leave their jobs to become an entrepreneur. What's your advice for them?

Khalia Collier: People have this thing about entrepreneurship. If you're starting a business to become a millionaire, you have the wrong motive. You should start a business to solve a problem, to see a need in the community. Then, money will come along with it. For me, it's sacrifices. You come last. When people make the decision to have kids, or when you have kids and you don't even see it coming, you have to know that selfishness is not an option. At that point, your job is to provide for your team. I took that really personal. Like, I will be the last one until we get this thing growing and building.

To look back on it, and to realize that I lived on $50 a month for food is craz. I had strategic lunch meetings because sometimes that would be my only meal of the day. I think when I finally decide to write a book, people will probably be really surprised to see that I was able to keep a smile on my face during some real, real dark moments.

It was hard. When you're building something, you have to trust people with your vision. You have to talk about what you're trying to accomplish with people because you know that things happen through people, but everyone didn't cherish that vision or didn't see what you saw. How did you deal with disappointments of people who you trusted?

You have to understand not everyone's going to share your vision. Not everyone's going to be ride or die for you. Not everyone's going to see what you see miles and miles ahead of you. That took a lot of lessons for me. You realize your circles grow smaller. You trust a little bit less. The ones that you know from your gut are the right type of people that need to be in your life; you keep those people and you discard the others that don't have your best interests at heart or aren't truly supportive.

As an entrepreneur, you take on so many risks, you take so much weight on your shoulders. To add anything else to that, you'll send yourself into a meltdown.

I had to have some alone, me time, to figure out what I wanted to accomplish and the type of people I wanted in my life was really important for me. To know that those sacrifices lead to an end goal. That's what's important.

The people who doubt you, you got to use it as fuel. You just don't have time to feed into that. Someone else's issues, fears, or reluctance to help; it has to stay theirs. They can't become yours because the only direction you're moving is forward.

Will you talk a little bit about the importance of building a culture? What are some things that you do as a leader to create a culture that's conducive to your goals?

Khalia Collier: I'm really big on culture. I'm big on cultural fits with our players. I'm big on cultural fits with our staff. A part of that is just being you. I have this thing: If I don't like you, I don't want to work with you. What I mean by that is if I don't naturally get a good feeling for you, I don't want to be in the office with you, depending on you. I don't want you in a part of our program if you're not just a good person. If we don't share the same values of the Golden Rule, of treat others the way you want to be treated and if I feel like that's not something that you represent or you're not someone I would trust to be around my family, you're not going to work for us, period. I'm really cut and dry on that.

Also, I've had the opportunity to sit down with so many leaders from millionaires to billionaires. I've been able to sit in executive staff and board meetings. I've had a lot of opportunities. I wanted to create something where people actually have fun. You know we're going to work really, really hard, but you can be chill, too. You don't always have to be on point to where you got to be dressed to the nines. We're an athletic team.

I like the fact that we can wear sweats in the office. But we know, when we need to dress up in slacks and a pencil skirt, we look the part. It's being able to do both. That's a part of the culture I build. You work hard. You play hard. But you know that you have to work harder to play harder. As long as you don't get those two switched around, you're in good hands.

What are some keys that young women need to know to be able to be successful in organizations these days? What are some of those tangible skills they need to have?

Khalia Collier: It's important for them to understand persistence, and that you're going to hear, "No." And how to handle that, how to navigate it, how to reposition yourself. Those are key things that I feel like aren't taught in school. You can't teach someone that they're going to struggle. You can't teach someone that they're going to experience failure. It's how you rebound from it. It's how you handle it. It's how you learn from it. That's what makes you a strong person.

We're seeing the next generation of women that are evolving. I think it's kind of cool. I brag about it, the fact that we have an all female internship. What's double-y cool is that they're working and their executive team is women. I know when I came out, all of my managers, my GMs, my president, my CEO were all older white men. To see that we're leading a franchise and we're 30 and under. We're a group of powerful, determined, young, tenacious women. I feel like that says something to where anything is possible. If you want to own your own team, if you want to be an attorney, you can.

We've heard countless times, over and over, we can do anything that we put our minds to. And it's true. If you let someone else stifle your dreams, shame on you. You got to go for it. To be able to put that in our staff from a culture standpoint of you're going to go for the best opportunity, and we're going to prepare you for it.

But we're not just going to prepare you from a textbook type of way. You're going to learn what initiative is. You're going to learn how to adapt. That's what life is. That's what sports is. For example, you get thrown into a three-two zone, but you thought they were in a man, guess what you do? You don't fold. You adapt. I think that's what's really cool.

We recruit athletes. I don't really care what type of athlete you are. I'm not biased to just basketball players. You just had to have some type of competitive nature in you to know that quitting is just not an option. I think that's one of the biggest things for young girls to know and young women to understand. What is your alternative? When you think about your alternative, and you know that it's not an alternative, then you're driving forward. It's literally that simple.

I get really, really geeked about the smallest things. I'm one of those people that believe in motivational quotes. You have to keep yourself motivated, and then, you have to keep others that motivate you, too. It can't just be you picking up everybody else. If you don't have someone that's feeding into you, too, it's going to be a long, long journey.

Having other people around to help you when things get tough is essential. I talked to some other people about not feeling ready. There women, who are athletes, who are doing these extraordinary things. We've all taken positions when we know, for a fact, we didn't know what we were doing. It took those people around us to help us.

What's some of the best advice that you've received from your mentors?

Khalia Collier: I've had so many different mentors, from all different areas, too. People like to just stick to, "I'm only going to be in sports, so I'm only going to know people in sports." In order for you to be a well-rounded individual, you want to seek out people from all different industries, all different levels of leadership.

One of the biggest things that I've seen from my female mentors is that they put in the work. I don't know one of them that haven't worked incredibly hard, that maintain the level of admiration, consistency. That's what they've really shared in me. You've got to be consistent. You can't just expect someone to write you a $100,000 check the day they meet you. That's not how relationships are built.

How have you stayed the course? I'm sure people have come to you and have offered you other opportunities.

Khalia Collier: Staying the course is hard. I've been very fortunate. I wanted something that's going to sustain me outside of Surge. I was making great money out of college. I didn't decide to own a women's basketball team because I was going to be a millionaire the next day. I did something that was strategic for me. I sought out a role that I knew would give me flexibility. That's what I do when I'm not with Surge. I lead an Institute for Private Business at St. Louis University. It's a great strategic position. I work with the top family privately owned businesses. Not only am I helping with their business growth, it's helping me with mine.

Staying the course is hard. When you're tempted with other six-figure positions. I've had the opportunity to go work with other sports franchises. But when I think back, I'm able to create my own. It's not someone else's vision. It's my vision. We're starting with a blank canvas. If we want to do something random at halftime, we have no one to tell us no. I think that's what keeps me here and building. I know what we're creating is unique. I know what we're creating is going to set the standard and really create the evolution of the next wave of women's sports.

I believe that down to my core. So, right now, there's not another six-figure job that can pop up. Those jobs will be there—if I decide to take a shift, or if I decide to do something else. I feel like Surge is my springboard for what's next, but it's something I want to keep growing and really take this model and build it across the country.

Just last year, I was looking at other options that were coming up. I was getting antsy. Five years has gone by fast. I'm 28 now. Do I want to take this corporate job? But I have a lot of fun doing what I do. It's a lot of long hours, but I'd rather be working 16 hour days for myself than for someone else.

People coming up have that same mentality. They want to be entrepreneurs. They want to do something for themselves. But it's important to remember that it has to be strategic. Strategy makes all the difference in the world.

I'm all about entrepreneurship until people don't understand you don't get paid vacation days. You do not have sick days. That is real. When you take time off from work, you're taking time off from your own growth. That's hard for a lot of people to swallow. Entrepreneurship sounds sexy until you realize, "You don't have any benefits?" No. There aren't benefits. You've got to figure out how to make it work.

What is your big vision for Surge and the Surge model?

Khalia Collier: I'm still wrapping my mind around what's possible. The Surge has continuously evolved year to year. What I envision the Surge becoming in the next five to ten years, I don't think half the people will understand. We haven't even reached the tip of our potential. The model that we're creating is unique within its own right.

We're recruiting a high I.Q. level of, not just basketball I.Q., but academic I.Q. to be able to really set women up for success outside of sports. That's what I'm really passionate about. Until we're at a level where we're signing multi-million dollar contracts right out of college, things will change. I'm not saying we're not going to get there. I hope that we get there within the next five to ten years, where you're seeing an exponential increase in female salaries in women's sports.

Until then, we're going to perfect out a model to be able to help players succeed once they're done playing. I have an agency I've been waiting to launch. I've got a consulting firm that I'm waiting to launch. Between NFL, MLB, we have so many different tie-ins to where we're going to show that our model not only works in women's sports but that it's transferable in men's sports. A lot of the times, people don't think those two cross paths. They very much so do. You don't have to sacrifice the person for the athlete just because of money. We're going to show that you can do that, and you can still win.

I think that's what's going to be cool. When people are like, "Oh, wow! We're recruiting the best of the best and we're blowing teams out the water."

Will you talk a little bit about the salaries of women athletes, which you mentioned some, but talk a little more about that? And how the Surge is providing opportunities, not in competition with the WNBA, but an alternative for women who want to play.

Khalia Collier: We are not a competition to the WNBA. We're simply a different model. It's still a lot of education that goes into women's sports. People see professional female athletes, and your mind wants to tell you they make multi-million dollar contracts. That's just not the reality. Seeing that the average WNBA salary still is pushing not even $60,000 yet, and you're still seeing the NBA average salary at $3 million. That's a hell of a gap, and it's not going to change overnight.

For a lot of women, a lot of people make it seem like overseas is just the end and the be all. As a female athlete, when you're at one, to two, to three Americans on each team, you're 16, 17 hours away from home. Maybe you don't want to play overseas. I don't think people factor that in. We're that alternative. Maybe you don't want to be across the world from your family, and you want them to be your support system at home.

We provide that alternative. Maybe you want to play in front of your family and friends. That other alternative is so key. A lot of female athletes feel like, "I got to keep playing, pursuing my passion, and playing ball." Or, "I got to stop playing ball and get a job." There's no in between. For us to create that in between is what I'm really, really passionate about.

There's such a big disconnect between men and women's sports that people still don't realize. I'm excited for the 20th anniversary of the WNBA because it is only going to grow. Women's sports is continuing to become more athletic, more entertaining. It's growing at another level because different generations are taking over.

That's what I'm excited about. When you think about what's next in our future, it's going to be really, really fun to watch. I think the WNBA has a huge opportunity to gain more momentum for the next 20 years. With new leadership coming into the WNBA, I'm really, really hopeful that she's going to be able to lead them to exponential growth, and they just build a powerhouse team that's been much needed to take the WNBA to a whole new level.

Are there any other team structures like the Surge in the country?

Khalia Collier: I can confidently say there's not another team structure like us across the country. We've done the research to show it. That is exactly what we're doing. We can't be on an island by ourselves. I'm hoping that we are setting that standard, that bar of excellence. Within the WBCBL, you're seeing it become more competitive. It's getting on more radars of not only female athletes but NCAA.

You're seeing pro teams acknowledging it as a separate professional development league. I want us to continue pioneering, trailblazing, and shattering glass ceilings that people didn't think you could. That puts us in a great spot. I smile because we only get better. When you think about that from the next wave of generation that's coming in, that's hungry, that has a fire under them, that's excited to just make some waves, we only get better.

We're watching it happen and making it happen. I think that's pretty cool for anyone that's a part of it, that's seeing it, that's just excited about it. What's cool is it doesn't just start with women. We're seeing a lot of men that's supporting the movement. You're seeing a lot of dads with daughters that want the same opportunities that they've had. That's steady growing. I always think that's special. We pay so much attention to just the women, but the guys have to be supporting the movement with us in order for it to work.

What are the final pieces of advice you would like to share with current female student-athletes?

Khalia Collier: You hear things are going to take time, but you don't really know what that means. Patience is key. A lot of people quit their businesses and other things before they even let them blossom. I don't want to start ten businesses. You've got to give things a chance to work even in the rough patches.

When the sun's not shining and it's super rainy, you've got to know that it's going to pass and that you've got to stick with your goal. If you're going to do this, you've got to stick with it. If it comes a point in time where you pivot, then you strategically pivot and you weigh all of your options before you do so.

Khalia Collier's Contact Information:
Facebook: St. Louis Surge Women's Basketball
Twitter: @stlsurge
Instagram: stlsurge
Website: www.stlsurgebasketball.com

Chapter 3: PASHA COOK

Current occupation: Empowerment speaker and coach for women and girls.

Where did you attend college and what sport did you play?

Pasha Cook: I played basketball and I was a point guard at the University of Memphis. However, I started out at a junior college.

What was that process (college recruiting process) like for you?

Pasha Cook: I actually got my first basketball scholarship at twenty-four. It was a long journey because I had an unstable childhood. I went to many, many schools and by the eleventh grade, I had lost my eligibility. I didn't have enough credits, so I couldn't play and I lost the hope of ever using my basketball skills to go to college, and so I dropped out.

Well, luckily while I was traveling from all these different schools, at one particular school, Alief Hastings High School, I met my principal and it was an unfortunate reason that I was in her office but she informally adopted me in that moment. She literally took me home and has been in my life ever since.

WNBA came along in ninety-six and I was just like, "Oh my God, I can play pro?" We had semi-pro teams in Houston, and I wanted to go try out and play with that team. I didn't have a car at the time because she said I need an education. She wanted me to get a GED, so I did it.

The same coach that I was trying to play for in a semi-pro team said, "Pasha, we're putting together the roster; what school did you attend?" I replied, "Home School University."

Because I hadn't gone to college, he said I couldn't play on the team. Instead, he took me under his wing and called a coach at the University of Mississippi who was interested. Then he drove me from Houston, Texas to Lafayette, Louisiana to play in a pickup game in front of the coaches and that day, I got my first basketball scholarship to Mississippi Gulf Coast Community College.

I finished up there and went on to play at the University of Memphis because some people who were on the team were from Memphis and it made me feel closer to home. More importantly, I became the first in my family to graduate.

Sports has changed my life completely and it took one transition after another to get there.

What was your major and why did you select that major?

Pasha Cook: Actually, I didn't select it. When I went over to the junior college, I was majoring in education but I was going on to become a physical therapist, so I thought. When I arrived at school, however, I realized that I was majoring in kinesiology because the practicum hours interfered with basketball and so it was disheartening, but I went with it.

I was happy to be playing and getting an education and so I went on to become a teacher for four years in Memphis, Tennessee before I branched off into entrepreneurship.

What was your first job when you finished college?

Pasha Cook: Since I majored in education, I kind of knew what was going to happen when I graduated. Education is a great field to be in and you know many great teachers are needed, but when you're in physical education, it's a different ballgame because coaches are usually former athletes and they don't leave those positions.

How important is networking?

Pasha Cook: You have to utilize your network. It's important to know who is on your team and keep in contact with people at your school. Building relationships with people outside of your school is very important when you're transitioning because those same people that you built those relationships with are going to be the first ones in line to help you.

With college sports, you're so busy that it's really hard at times to network. That's why it has to be a focus for you because it's easy to get distracted with school, athletics, and all these other things that are going on around you. You really have to set out to do that. It's not just going to happen.

What are some strategies that can be used to build meaningful relationships?

Pasha Cook: There're many, many ways. I mean we can't get to all of them right now but for a short synopsis, they're people that come to your games. Maybe, instead of going hang out with your friends, one weekend, you decide to set a lunch with somebody and have a conversation because there's a mentorship opportunity. It could be someone you admire such as a businessperson, or community leader that could offer wisdom.

In college programs, people within the community, especially business owners, are at the games. They're involved with the school in some kind of way. It's a win-win relationship if you connect with them.

Figure out who's out there, who you feel like can teach you what they've learned and set a lunch with them. The little breaks you do have, you have to focus and be intentional to build those lasting relationships. You can go online platforms such as LinkedIn and Facebook, and start being a part of groups that focus on the area in which you have a desire to learn more about. They'll let you know what's going on in your community.

What's an example of how networking helped you?

Pasha Cook: In 2013, I moved to New York. I think my family thought I was crazy because I was giving up this great job and I had the life that most people would have settled for. I know I was doing really well, but something was calling me. I wasn't living my passion. I didn't have basketball anymore and I hadn't found that passion, so I went through transition, after transition, after transition.

I came to New York to work in the fashion industry and did a four-month internship with a celebrity stylist who worked with athletes. The stylist didn't hire me once the internship ended so I had to figure what I was going to do from there because I needed money.

Those four months I'd been working for free. I was going to start working for Sachs 5th Avenue in a couple of weeks and was finding my niche in the luxury retail market.

Well, the stylist that I had been working for called me and said, "Oh my God, I don't know why I didn't think of you. I need you to show up."

I said, "Well, what do you need me to do?" She replied, "I have a gig for you." I thought it's wardrobe styling. It was presenting a transition workshop at the WNBA! Now, I've been doing the presentation the last three years. I was there for the 20th anniversary.

Being persistent, trusting the universe and trusting my gut feeling resulted in me being a part of the WNBA without being a player.

Why did you keep pursuing your passion even though everyone else thought you were crazy?

Pasha Cook: I don't like when people try to put me in a box. But once I started to grow in confidence and believe in the people who believed in me, then I started to remove the boxes out of my life. If someone is telling me I can't do something, especially when I have a passion for it, I block them out.

My family knows this and they don't try anymore. I'm not going to listen to someone on the outside because my family supports me. They may not understand, but they'll go silently and support me and they know that I'm going to get it done. I'm going to make it happen.

How did playing sports, in particular, basketball, impact like your approach to life?

Pasha Cook: Well, being able to go and play at the age that I was able to play and prosper showed me that I had something special inside of me. Sports just elevated that.

Sports helped me to be disciplined with time because we had a tough schedule and every place had a time that you had to be there. It wasn't necessarily time management, rather time focus. I learned how to focus my time.

Again, sports taught me to be disciplined. So as an entrepreneur, I can get up anytime, but I usually get up between the hours of four and six at the latest every morning, and even during weekends. I always have a routine going.

Sports have done so much for me. It's just really helped me to have those transferable skills, which I talk about with athletes to identify those transferable skills and know that if you can become an athlete at the collegiate level, you can do anything because it takes a lot to get there.

Being able to focus and balance so many things is a skill that's necessary for life. What do you have to constantly manage and balance on a day-to-day basis?

Pasha Cook: First, I have to manage and balance my mind because my mind is always going. Whether I'm trying to figure out something that I didn't do right, learn a lesson, or create something new for tomorrow, I have to always balance my mind.

I do that through meditation—which really has helped me to really get what people call "cool." Someone told me, "You're like this wall and if something, you throw a ball, it's just going to bounce off you."

I'm thinking, "Yeah, you didn't know me maybe just five years ago."

But understand this, in order to be great at something, you have to fail at something else. That's why you need to know what your values are because you can't give a hundred percent to everything. You cannot, so you have to figure out what is balance for you. You have to define what balance is for you. You can't let other people define that.

How do you find balance and know when enough is enough?

Pasha Cook: Your body tells you. Athletes should know how to listen to their bodies. Your body is going to tell you when it needs sleep. Your body is going to tell you when you're dehydrated.

Your body is going to tell you when there is something going on inside of you that you need to go get checked out. Your body is going to tell you when you've had enough.

However, you don't want it to get to that point. You have to learn how to feed you first. You have to learn how to feed you first and take care of you first.

Once you come out of sport, it is even more important. While you are playing, you have people there telling you what to do, when to do it, how to be in shape. You've got trainers working you out.

You have to transfer that into this life and still take care of your body because you're probably going to have more injuries than the average person, too. You know ailments.

Just start taking care of your body and figure out what you need. For me now, it's more yoga, elliptical because I've had several surgeries.

Taking care of yourself is especially important for young women. What are some ways that women can do a better job of taking care of themselves?

Pasha Cook: It's unfortunate that women have been conditioned to play a supporting role. This made sense in the cavemen time when men were out hunting, you know, dinosaurs or whatever and killing for food. They had to survive, right? But this is a different world in 2016. Women are single mothers; there's so much going on in the world today that we have to adjust to the new world and the new world is saying, "Go out and get your dreams!"

We no longer have to hunt. The cows are already there grazing. We don't have to hunt anymore, right? Some people hunt for recreation. Nevertheless, women have learned to be supportive and that's fine. We need to support other people, but women didn't learn how to support themselves.

As a result, some women, when they try to support a dream or something that they want to do, they have this guilty feeling of not being there for other people. They don't realize that if you don't know how to be there for you, then what you're giving out isn't a hundred percent and it's not coming from a positive energy anyway.

Here's an example, think of this cup representing you as a woman. When it gets full and it starts to overflow and it goes into the saucer, that's what you give to other people. Women need to learn how to do that and to understand that their dreams matter, that we're not in the caveman days anymore.

What was a turning point for you where you knew that it was time to start looking after Pasha and going after your dreams without sacrificing so much for others?

Pasha Cook: Well, you know that's a day-to-day thing. I still have the conditioning of my DNA. I still have the conditioning of my ancestors who were here way before me, so we still have that it's just you get up every day, determine to do your best and to give you your best.

Showing up for myself first.is a daily regime for me. Some days I show up ready to go and there're some days it's like "uhhh." It's daily, but as far as the turning point, I think when I decided to come to New York, that was the turning point.

I had two huge turning points in my life. One was to go off to college. I had never been out of Texas. I had to leave Texas for Mississippi. I watched all the movies about Mississippi before I got there, which was a mistake.

Then deciding to stretch myself, I knew New York would stretch me. I knew it would and I came anyway and I started to see what was really on the inside of me.

I had to figure out, "How do I handle this atmosphere?" and it made me start to focus on the inside. As a result, I also got a therapist— which, in our culture, has this negative connotation to it, but I had a therapist—and she started having me to read stuff like Eckhart Tolle. That was one of the first books she recommended, The Power of Now.

That switched on a light bulb for me and I started being more in the personal development space. I wanted to know more about myself, learning more about myself, and realized I wanted to know more about how other people function. That launched a whole personal development transition for me.

What impact did stepping outside of your comfort zone have on your life?

Pasha Cook: I'm a lot further than I have ever been in my life, so I understand that in order to get to where I see I want to go, I have to be uncomfortable. We all will have these moments in our lives where it feels like everything is coming in on us and you realize this is a breakthrough moment.

For example, as you're going up a threshold, you have turbulence and then you get up above the clouds and you're good. Then when you rise to another level, you have to go through it again because it's building your strength—it's a muscle.

It's a muscle to challenge yourself through your fears. It's a muscle to challenge yourself and be okay with the uncomfortable part of your life knowing that there's something bigger than you that's helping you. You just got to have that focus. I've seen it happen so much.

Give an example of when you've gone to that next level and what was that for you?

Pasha Cook: Well, New York was that next level. Moving three times in one year, interning in the snow. I'm from Texas, I'm not used to being in knee deep snow out here and walking a half mile to a train and all these kind of things just to go to the store or just to go to work. That was the next level of discomfort for me—and getting to know this city, not being afraid of what I've seen and watched on television.

When I was interning, I did feel like I was being punked at times. I have to tell you because she had me doing some things I didn't expect. I thought somebody was going to jump up from behind a tree and tell me I was being punked because this couldn't be true.

I was thinking, "I know I'm not walking a mile with all these clothes in my hand." That really stretched me. I probably talked to my therapist more often, the first couple of years. If you can make it in New York and make a name for yourself, you definitely can make it anywhere else.

It's like being in college sports after coming from high school or going into pro sport. Everybody is at that level, so what are you going to do differently?

What are the final pieces of advice you would like to share with current female student-athletes?

Pasha Cook: You have to go back to what helped you to become a successful athlete. Even if you were riding the bench and you made it to college, something helped you to get there. Find out what that is and implement it in what you want and you're going to be okay.

If you want to champion your life, give me a call; I'm going to help you. I promise. I'll be publishing my first book this year so look for that in December. It's entitled Unrepeatable Miracle. It's just showing women, girls, and anyone who reads it how to turn your struggles into your strengths regardless of your background. No matter what family you were born into, you can still discover your inner champion and champion your life!

Pasha Cook's Contact Information:
Email: info@pashacook.com
Facebook: www.facebook.com/pashacooktv
Twitter: @Pasha Cook
Instagram: PashaCook
Website: www.pashacook.com

Chapter 4: OSA OSULA

Current occupation: Middle School Physical Education teacher.

Where did you attend college and what sport did you play?

Osa Osula: I went to George Mason University and I played basketball.

What was your greatest accomplishment in your athletic career?

Osa Osula: I would have to say our freshman class definitely helped to establish the George Mason team. We went to the WNIT our first year being there, then again we made it back to the WNIT our last year. I feel like our freshman class really helped to contribute towards our university.

What was your major and why did you select your major?

Osa Osula: I majored in communications and George Mason is known for our communications program, so it was almost a no-brainer for me to want to learn more about it.

My specialty is actually public relations. I was always so curious as to how to put a spin on someone's scandal. Also being able to see what might be happening with a person's life and how to put a positive spin on it. I was so intrigued by that, so I went into communications.

What factors impacted your decision on your current career path and what are you doing now?

Osa Osula: Okay. I'm a physical education teacher right now so it has nothing to do with communication. Actually, it has a little to do with communication. I decided to go on a different career path. I winded up getting hurt playing basketball overseas and when I got back, I was no longer in the Virginia area. Coming back to New York and not having a professional network and it was very hard to get my foot in the door for communications.

I just decided to go back to school and I started to pursue physical therapy. After taking out loans for $18,000 I realized I kind of like kids. I took a couple physical education electives and I just absolutely loved it. I never really looked back after that.

What is it about kids that you love?

Osa Osula: One of the things I love about children is that they are, and this is just my take on it; they're just not far removed from God. I feel like they just have this awesome connection. They are just totally being themselves and I love learning from them.

I know everybody thinks just because you're a teacher, you're supposed to be teaching them and mentoring them, but I learn so much from kids. I learn how not to be fearful of everything because I think as we become adults, you just become so bogged down in fear and what if I do this, what if I do that. Kids don't behave that way.

They do it and they see if they get in trouble and they move on from there.

I feel like there's just so much to be learned from them. They bring out the best in people and I'm just grateful that I have that experience because my day is never the same. I don't know what I'm going to walk into each day, which is something that I love.

How did you secure your first job after college playing basketball overseas?

Osa Osula: I knew that I wanted to play basketball after college. In college, my coach's strategy was everybody had a role. Everybody did their role well. My role was to rebound, block shots, play good defense.

Coming out of college, I didn't have all the points that everybody had because that was not my job on my team. It just made trying to play overseas that much harder, but I knew that was something that I wanted to do.

I found an "agent" online. It would later turn out to be a pretty bad decision on my part. She basically told me I would have to pay her $750 up front. I would buy my own ticket to go and play overseas. They would have some tournament that I could play in and showcase my skills. When it is something that you want so badly, it's so easy for you to fall into the hype and the trap of people who just solely want to make money.

Anyway, I paid it. I flew overseas. I played in Holland in this tournament where a team saw me and decided that they wanted to bring me over for a tryout on their team. Nevertheless, I still had two classes that I had to finish in college.

My plan was to go try out and if the team really wanted me, they would fly me back from Virginia to go and play in Germany. The agent, who I will leave nameless on here, basically said, "Go; this is a good opportunity. Go and try out."

Like an idiot, I decided to do that against my better judgement because I just had this dream. I was like, "Oh my God, this dream is coming true. This is going to be total like the movie *Love and Basketball*." I think that was what we all aspired to.

I stayed and I only had about weeks' worth of clothes. I let another person derail my plan because I thought she knew more than I did.

I went and tried out for the team. They told me it was going to be about a week or two-week tryout and they'd fly me back to the states. I did not get anything in writing and I just believed what they said. I mean, you would not even believe half of the workout plan. Now that I think about all the things I had to do prior to trying out for this team, I would've just been like deuces guys. Keep your money and I'll just fly home.

I winded up getting hurt and then, of course, we had to play in a basketball game. The team decided that I was too skinny, even though they saw me in Holland so they knew my size. Again, they just said that I was too skinny.

At this point, I had hated all Germans and I was ready to just go to jail at that point. Thankfully, I had a wonderful angel on my side who talked me out of it. Her name was Angie Lewis. She said, "No, we don't know the laws here and we can't do all this stuff." I was said, "mm-hmm (negative) girl, somebody's going down."

Long story short, I didn't kill anyone and I didn't destroy any property. I didn't go to jail or any of that stuff, but I wanted to because I was that pissed off.

The reason why I was so upset is because they decided that they were going to give me 50 Euros and send me back to Holland. I' told them, "That wasn't the deal. You told me you were going to fly me back home."

During this time, Angie was such a big help to me because she said, "Don't worry. Everything's going to work out. I have an agent. I'll put you in contact with her. She actually lives in Germany." I thought to myself, "No. All Germans are horrible, they can't be trusted." I was so extreme with a lot of my commentary when I was young.

Angie winded up hooking me up with that agent who was very reliable. She let me live with her. She had a team for me to try out for the next day. I needed time to put myself together and remember that this was a dream of mine. I decided I was going to make this happen!

After wiping away all the tears and trying out, I made that team. The agent told me the coach liked to see people smiling. She continued, "Go there, smile, play some good basketball and you'll be fine."

Thankfully, I was finally able to call my parents and let them know I made the team. My parents didn't want me to go overseas and try out, but I went anyway. With all of this happening, they would've killed me along the way. I contacted my parents, told them everything that happened. I also contacted my sister and she was able to fly out, bring me some clothes. At that point, there was just no way for me to go back.

In addition, I needed to reach out to my professors so I could finish school. I still had a few classes left and didn't want to lose that credit. Thankfully, they let me take the classes as independent studies.

I say all of this to say that you have to be very careful with your decision making because some people are not honest. I think just going from college where people did a lot of things for us and we just assume that everybody's honest is not the case. That's my story.

What made you shift your identity from being only an athlete?

Osa Osula: I think after getting injured while playing basketball, it just kind of put things in perspective for me. I realized that I can't do this forever. It helped me to also understand that basketball's such a small part of who I am and what I do.

I needed to really get honest with myself and get honest with where I wanted to be in the next three years. I just don't think that I really gave that enough thought while I was in college.

I realized that now that I'm removed from basketball, nobody cares. Nobody cares that I went to George Mason and I played. Nobody cares that I played overseas and that's fine. I'm totally okay with that.

Can you think of a time when you made a mistake and how you bounced back from it?

Osa Osula: A big mistake was not fact-checking the person who claimed to be an agent. The one thing that I learned from this process of wanting to go overseas is you should never pay somebody upfront. If an agent is offering you a service you simply give your name, give your height, give your stats or your basketball resume and you don't have to pay anything upfront.

Their job is to collect money from the team that they send you to. Nobody told me that. I just was thinking, "Oh, I got to find an agent. What do I do?" I literally typed in agent on Google and found someone.

Another lesson is, if you bought a ticket to fly to one of those overseas camps that everybody's claiming to have now, and the team wants you, you fly back home. Afterwards, if a team really wants you that bad, they will fly you back and you won't have to worry about what you will have to do if a team cut you.

I think those two things are really important to know. Don't listen to people who have never played overseas. Playing overseas was so glorified. They made it seem like there was this glamorous experience and meanwhile I'm riding a bike an hour and a half to practice every day. Not to say that there's anything wrong with that. I did it for two years because I loved the game that much, but people need to be honest about what your true experience is. Everybody's experience is obviously different, but if I had to do it all over again, I'm not really sure I would've stayed two years.

What else are you now passionate about outside of work and basketball?

Osa Osula: I started a YouTube channel and it's still young. I'm going on my second year in July, but it's my pride and joy. It's my baby. One of the things that I love about this new venture is that I don't wake up every morning sore. I don't have any injuries. I don't have a sprained wrist because I was applying eye shadow the wrong way.

I never thought I would be able to love something as much I used to love basketball. I talk about spirituality and dating. I talk honestly about my dating experiences as a 34-year-old woman in New York. I talk about hair, makeup and I also do my hair and makeup while I'm on that channel. It's so therapeutic.

I love the fact that it's creating community for other women. Especially other black women who can and relate to my experiences. There're so many 30 something-year-olds who are struggling in love just like I am.

What are some examples of the ways that you've used your background in sports in your day-to-day life?

Osa Osula: Sports taught me about having integrity and having a great work ethic. That just shows up for me every single day. I've always been an upfront, honest, and loyal person.

I had one of the best AAU coaches in the world. He just taught me that who you are on the court is who you are off the court. I live by that.

Sometimes I find it hard to have a balance with other people who haven't played sports because they don't live by the same code. Most of my friends are athletes because we live within the same code. I very rarely have any issues with them because I feel like they understand how to be in a sisterhood and they understand how to be a team player. They understand what it truly means to have a connection, a relationship, and a friendship. You need all those things when you're playing this game.

What are some skills that you would say are most transferable and necessarily for young women now who are graduating from college? What should they know how to do?

Osa Osula: First and foremost, you should know how to advocate for yourself. Ask for the things that you want. Ask for the things that you need because nobody is going to be able to read your mind. You should have an idea of where you want to be.

What are your goals? What do you want to actually accomplish? You can't just sit back and think that things are going to just drop into your lap because that's not how life works. Again, especially if you don't have any desire of playing basketball after college, you have to really get focused.

I feel like I'm lucky because I'm doing a job that I'm passionate about. It doesn't feel like work. I have this other leisure activity I can do on YouTube and stuff like that. It's nice.

There is such pressure to never stop or take breaks which can cause a lot of stress. How do you de-stress and manage all that you have going on?

Osa Osula: I have a lot of things that I love to do. First and foremost, I always take care of myself. I love looking good. I love smelling good and I love feeling good. I'm not trying to die early. I'm not trying to keep up with the "Joneses." I've never been that person. I don't feel those same stresses as someone else might be feeling. You should not be comparing yourself to anyone else. This is your life. This is the only life you have so if you're not making the best of it, then it's all in vain. You're wasting your time.

What are the final pieces of advice you would like to share with current female student-athletes?

Osa Osula: You should be getting enough rest. You should be taking care of yourself so that you can think straight, so you can feel good. When I'm centered the best, things come forth. I feel like I am so much more creative that way. When I'm thinking of 101 things at one time, I can't get myself together. You have to be in a place of peace in order to be as creative as possible.

My page on YouTube is Living with Osa. You can learn about your hair. You can learn about makeup. My 20 something-year-olds should watch the dating series so they can just gain some insight because if I knew the things that I know now back then, it would be a completely different story.

Osa Osula's Contact Information:
Email: info.osaosula@gmail.com
Twitter: @LivingWithOsa
Instagram: LivingWithOsa
YouTube: Living with Osa

Chapter 5: MARISA GONZALEZ

Current occupation: Director & U18 Girls Head Coach of Noria F.C. soccer Club.

Where did you go to college and what sport did you play?

Marisa Gonzalez: I'm from Pueblo, Mexico and I played soccer at Southwest Minnesota State University.

When did you start playing soccer and how did your love for the game ultimately get you to the US to play at the university level?

Marisa Gonzalez: I started young. I was around seven or eight years old when I started playing. Like many girls, I started playing with boys. I guess you have to have a certain type of personality to do that. I never cared. Obviously, I was a tomboy, so I was fine with it.

By 12, I started playing with girls and we started getting pretty good. When I was 14, I was playing on the pre-National team. At this time, the National team did not have under-17, 15 or 13. It was just the National team, so I didn't want to pursue that. It was just too much of a gap in age difference between the players since most of them were in their 30's and I was 14. As a result, I figured I should try college soccer.

In 1998, my soccer team from Mexico went Minnesota to play in a tournament. That's when I decided that I want to play college soccer in the US. I knew without a doubt that's what I want to do.

I had to be 15 to 18, I just did everything I could to play soccer in the US, which was a lot harder back then than it is now. I lived in Mexico, and we didn't have YouTube or Skype or anything. I started thinking, "How am I going to get them to see me? I'm so far away." I worked with my parents and just did a lot of research.

You reached out to different coaches? How did you and your parents make that happen?

Marisa Gonzalez: Well, I started researching what I needed to do. The internet was pretty new and slow back then. It is so different now. It wasn't that long ago, but technology has come a long way. I started going to websites. I started going into college websites. I started learning about NCAA, how it worked and I just started sending a lot of emails.

I created my resume and just started reaching out. I wrote, "I'm a soccer player from Mexico, what can I do? I want to go there. I'm interested in doing it, what can I do? How should I do it? Let me know." There was not a lot of information then, so that's what I did, send a lot of emails and just hope that someone would answer.

You were relentless. What was your process?

Marisa Gonzalez: Yeah, I just went after it. I had no idea what I was doing. I'll be honest. No idea. I had to do my video and send it out.

This is funny because again there was no YouTube, you had to record it and send the tape (VHS).

I realized, "Okay, I cannot send 150 tapes because I don't have the money for it." I would have to FedEx internationally each one of them. It was thinking, "Oh-oh, what should I do?" In moments like these, you start choosing based on what you think makes sense. For example, this coach is not that interested, so you will just discard that coach at that university because you couldn't do it.

When you finally found a university that you wanted to attend, how did you select a major?

Marisa Gonzalez: I always had a sense of the world. I have friends all over. I knew it had to be international something. Plus, I was an international student in the US who already spoke English, though not all that well. At first, I thought I would major in International Relations. Of course, I imagined I'd be this ambassador, why not?

My first year, I realized I'm not that interested in politics. Also, I'm not that good at doing politics. I'm very direct and it doesn't work in politics. No business, I thought. So, my sophomore year I transferred colleges and I switched majors.

I majored in International Business, which was great. It was right for me. A lot of times I'm doing a lot of coaching now and I tell people that it's okay to switch majors. It's okay if you're not ready or if you made a mistake. The thing is, you're going to be working the rest of your life. Just be certain that it's the right thing for you at that time. If it isn't something you used immediately, you didn't waste a year studying this or that, you just learned something else.

You mentioned also that you transferred schools; why did you transfer?

Marisa Gonzalez: My idea for transferring was completely sports related. I was not happy with the team. I was not happy with the coach. College was fine and I was happy in school. Just the coach was not giving me what I needed.

We had a small team and I had to play injured. I started having back injuries, which I still kind of scary. It got to the point where I couldn't walk and I was not treated. I was going to the trainer, but they were saying I probably wanted to get out of conditioning. So they were just giving me ice to wrap around my ankles.

When I came home in December, I went to my doctor and he said, "You were a week away from surgery in both ankles." I realized this was not right. I was suffering, because I was injured. They weren't listening and I was not enjoying playing soccer at the time.

I was mad. I was frustrated. I was pissed at everyone because I wasn't happy. I was injured. I was in pain and then I realized, he also wasn't paying attention to how I was doing academically. They didn't know what my classes were and they had no idea what was going on in my life. I decided I was going to transfer. I went and looked for a team that had more of what I wanted.

That sounds like it was a difficult situation. How did you decide where to transfer?

Marisa Gonzalez: It was hard because I was an international student, injured, not getting treated and I'm sure I was even depressed at one point. In this situation, I was by myself because my parents were hours away and many miles away. I had no idea what to do. I thought, "I'm going to transfer to either Minnesota or California."

I have family in California and Minnesota. I went and played USA Cup in 1998 in Minnesota. They became pretty much my family too. I went back to the house every year. I thought, if something like the situation I had before happens again, I would have someone an hour or two away, that can help me out. They would just be there for me and say, "This is going on, or this is not well."

I looked at those places and just again started emailing the coaches. After I got my release from that university, I started talking to coaches and I was lucky enough to talk to the one I had during college.

You just went after it again? Were you able to get your major there and have a much better experience?

Marisa Gonzalez: Yeah exactly, it was a great experience. Great team. Great coach. It was just a lot of fun.

What are some of your greatest accomplishments or memories as an athlete?

Marisa Gonzalez: To me, college was a whole experience, because I enjoyed it. It was hard. After that injury, my sophomore year it didn't go away and I was still injured. We worked at getting me back in shape. I didn't get that much playing time. It was a little frustrating, but the team was good and the team was fun. The whole experience was fun; even if you weren't playing that much, just because the team got along, it made a difference. To me, it was probably just being in the Finals of the conference tournament, which was a lot of fun.

When I was in high school, we made it to state and regionals, playing the pre-national team. I got to play against the national team three or four times with my club team. It was weird because you were playing much older players.

If someone plays soccer, they know Maribel Dominguez. She was the Mia Hamm in Mexico. I got to play against her I think four or five times. I had to mark her. I remember one time she was running around and I just grabbed her and I said, "Please stop. Just stop running. I can't do it anymore." She was just laughing. I was like, "You're too good."

What are some similarities and differences between playing in Mexico and then playing college here in the US?

Marisa Gonzalez: It's totally different because the US is just more evolved. It's more professional. You have trainers. You have state of the art facilities. You have weightlifting coaches. You have everything, just there for you to be a great athlete.

You have everything. Here, in Mexico, you have to find it. I was lucky enough to have great facilities and great coaches, but there's not that much competition. In the US, everything is through associations. Here, the association has this guy who's doing their own thing and they're a million leagues out. They're not federated. That's not that much competition. It makes a great deal when you can't find competition, when you can't find right coaches. Culture is a great thing, especially the soccer here federate.

Mexico is old school type of culture, especially moms, they don't want their kids playing soccer. They don't want their kids playing sports. You see a lot of girls, they don't play sports, not as they should be.

They have a boy and the first thing they start doing is, start finding soccer, baseball, football, whatever is cool for them. They have girls, they don't do that. The girl doesn't do that. It's changing that culture. Sports in general, I find it more competitive there. The cool American culture, they're competitive, very competitive. Here, it's not that much especially with girls. Here, you have to make them competitive. You have to make them want it.

When you don't have everything well organized, or just great facilities, it's a lot harder to do it. You have to just try to do your best. You have to do it because you want to do it. You have to work through it for if you want to go to college there.

How have you've used what you've learned in sports in your career path? Once you finished college, what did you do? How did you use sports?

Marisa Gonzalez: To me, I always tell people that I learned more in the sports than in the classroom. I tell everyone this. I don't remember chemistry. I don't remember anything of it. I remember what I learned in the sports.

First of all I learned teamwork. Teamwork is very important in the workplace, very important. If you do not get along with your boss, if you don't know how to work with them, or if you have people working under you, you don't know how to be a great boss, you're going to have a hard time working.

Teamwork was number one. Being passionate. And this comes again with choosing your career path correctly. Just do what makes you happy. Don't think about money. Don't think about being famous. Don't think about it's harder to do, just be happy with it and you'll be passionate. If you choose the right career path, you're going to do great, just because you have that passion. You have that commitment and discipline to do it.

After college, I did my Masters. After that, I started working events. I did Pan American Games with their championships and I worked 9:00 in the morning till 4:00 in the morning, non-stop, 16 hour shifts.

You worked from 9:00 am to 4 until 4:00 am every day?

Marisa Gonzalez: Yeah. I worked like that for two, three or four months at a time. I worked Saturdays and Sundays. For people that like watching Rio, trust me, they are suffering. People working in Rio now are not sleeping much.

Athletes don't see that part, but people behind the scenes work so much. You have discipline. You don't quit. That comes from sports. You don't quit. Its 4:00 in the morning, you're still there, because the team needs you. You have to do to get it done.

It doesn't matter what it is. That's a lot of the sports order. Just a lot of things I've learned from sports to what I do. Now I coach, so obviously everything I learned from sports I'm doing it, or tell me to do it.

To me, it was passion, great teamwork, which a lot of companies look for. When you're an athlete, you think everyone is a good team working and that's not true. If all my friends that did not do sports hate working on a team, it's unfair to them because some of them work more, some of them work less. On a team, if someone's injured, and t running you run for them. You do what has to be done to achieve the goal. It doesn't matter who did less or more. It has to get done.

What are the most important aspects of getting it done on a team?

Marisa Gonzalez: Just do whatever has to be done. It doesn't matter if you work harder, or if you did more than that person. The end result is the ultimate goal and what matters most.

A lot of discipline and competitive spirit, which is hard to find in girls sometimes, but be competitive. It doesn't mean I'm going to do whatever it takes to take everyone down. It means I'm going to do whatever it takes to be better. Competitive with myself. Work every day just to be a better person, professional, whatever you chose to do.

What are some challenges you face as you change careers? What are some mistakes that you've made as well that you've bounced back from?

Marisa Gonzalez: Mistake, probably my biggest one was, I did not stay in the US a year after I graduated. Was it a mistake? I already had a visa, I had permission. I could've stayed 1-year doing internships. I came home. Everything was so pretty and everyone was so nice. It was a mistake because I had an opportunity to be there another year and learn something else.

One of the greatest challenges was, the first was, coming out of college realizing you know nothing. Then your expectations versus reality are completely different things. I don't want to just kill people's dreams, but when you come out of college and you think it will be like television. You're a lawyer or doing pre-law and you want to be that guy working in New York City. You are a doctor, pre-med and you want to be like Grey's Anatomy.

That's not real. It's not how things work. You have this expectation, you come out and you're like, "They're not going to hire me, just because I'm nice." I got to have work experience, so just finding that whole thing was hard. I started working in a construction business. It was not my thing. We did soccer fields and we did baseball fields, but I'm not good at sales. I wasn't happy. Since you're not playing sports anymore like you used to you have to answer the questions, who I am? What I'm doing? Where do I go from here?

A lot of girls I used to coach, back in the day, are now graduating from college. I actually talked to one of them a few days ago. She just graduated; I'm like, "What are you going to do?" She's like, "No idea. I have no idea." I'm like, "It sucks, doesn't it?"

All of your life you're being told what to do. After elementary school, junior high, high school and then you go to college. After college, it's like, "Well now what?" I can work. I can go get married. I can do a Master's degree. I have so many options and nobody is telling me what to do. It's hard. That's the greatest challenge. It was, "where do I go from here?"

Especially, I went for business, which is so broad. You can do so much with it. I had no idea. I like marketing, but I didn't go to school for marketing. I like advertising, but I didn't go to school for that. I'm in business. Finance not so much, accounting not so much. I was throwing those away. I wouldn't like numbers that much.

I was thinking, "Oh my God, what do I do?" It took me two years to realize what I wanted to do. It wasn't right away. I worked here, I worked there. It was okay. I was just coping with it. Then it took a conversation with a friend that made me realize this master's degree sounds pretty cool. I think this is what I'm going to do and it was working in sports.

Not as an athlete because I was done, but it was doing the whole thing in the back. I went for a master's degree in Sports Administration in Madrid. I lived in Madrid for a year. Not bad.

How did you find that program in Madrid and why did you decide to pursue that degree?

Marisa Gonzalez: The friend I talked to, I talked to him at a party. He had just graduated from that Masters degree program. He played for the same club in I played in soccer. He also played in the US and then he went to Madrid. He was telling me about it. It was a Real Madrid school. He's telling me, "I'm doing this. Now I'm living in New York City. I'm working at the MLS. This is how I did it."

He started telling me the program. I was like, "It sounds really cool. I think I want to do this." I then talked to my parents, because I didn't have any money to pay for my Masters. I told my dad, , "I really want to do this, can you pitch in." He looked at it and went, "Yep, last thing I'm going to pay for you, but it's worth it."

I was lucky enough that they helped me out. They helped me out in everything, college too. I was lucky. I didn't have any loans. I didn't owe any money after college, so it helped a lot. I did my Masters and I focused on marketing and organizing sporting events and that's what I did.

Most players you don't think about everything that it takes to make an event happen. What does the operations side of sporting events entail?.

Marisa Gonzalez: Yeah it's crazy. People have no idea what it takes. I tell people when you see State competitions, Rio, London, whatever, every chair is there for a reason. That's what operations do. Every water break, everything is there for a reason. It takes so many people to organize things, especially when it's aired on TV. You have TV, you have award ceremony, you have everything going on and it's a monster. For example, one of my events, there was probably 300- 500 people working the event. That includes staff, volunteers, federations, TV and just everyone.

That's a lot of people to coordinate and to put together. Some of the young women that I've talked to asked how you deal with conflict. Managing 300 - 500 people, I'm sure there's conflict occasionally. How do you deal with that?

Marisa Gonzalez: To be honest, I'm not that good at it. I try to listen. Listening is my number one goal. When you're in that kind of an event, when there's a lot of pressure, because there's a lot going on.

When I did Pan American Games, I used to have three cell phones and my radio. They will all go off at the same time. You have so much stuff. You have conflict and you have everything that could go wrong just go wrong at the event. To me, it's listening. Listen to what they're saying. Listen to what's going on and then comprehend before reacting.

That's a really good point. That's a really great point—listening and taking the time to actually understand what the other person is saying before you jump in and be reactive. It sounds like that's one of the skills that young women need to be able to be successful once they leave college. What other skills would you say are absolutely critical to their success?

Marisa Gonzalez: Not only reacting, listening is very important. I think one has to just be more rationale sometimes. As an athlete, you're very passionate, but that rationale part, the whole take time, just see what options you have and just slow down a little bit. It's very important to slow down.

Athletes are in the moment so much and they're trained to react and respond. You're not trained to sit back and watch and evaluate, because you don't have time to, right?

Marisa Gonzalez: You don't have time. I always tell the girls I coach now, when you're playing soccer, if you make a mistake, you have one or two seconds to realize what you're going to do. Fix it and learn from it. In life, it's not that bad. When you're working, you have a little more time. Take it, analyze it. Analyze your options, analyze what you're going to do.

I would say have a plan. Just have a plan. I had the opportunity to take a leadership class. I think it was last semester. We talked about just having plans and having objectives, weekly objectives every time and writing it down. Just make sure you know how you're going to get where you want to get because we do it as athletes.

You know if you want to get better, you go to the gym. You eat better, you know how to do it. In life, it's just the same. How are you going to get there? Make the plan and make your objectives.

Number one you can grade them. Don't just say, "I'm going to go to the gym," or when you're an athlete, say, "I'm going to go to the gym three times a week from this time to this time." If you want to do a job, you want to learn a job, don't say, "I'm going to send my resume away." No, say "I'm going to interview with this company, this company, and this company. I'm going to send my resume to this person and this person," and make it accountable if you didn't do it at the end of the week. Be accountable for what you want to do.

Things just don't come. If you're walking up, maybe one thing will come, but you have to work for them, you have to be there and you have to work on your objectives. Just be clear and slow down.

Also don't be frustrated. Don't be frustrated, the whole thing. You have to fail a million times for one thing to work out. Yes it's true. A lot of people will say no and especially after college. You send your resume to maybe 500 or 600 people and you get 600 no's.

Just keep doing it. If it doesn't come, try to analyze, what do you have to do to make it happen. Maybe a career path. Maybe you have to go to school a little more. Maybe your resume is just not right for you. Maybe they don't like your resume. Maybe you're not working it right.

Sell yourself when you're looking for a job. Yeah, those are important too, I would say. To me, it's just, be rationale. Conflict, listen, take it in, analyze it and realize that you're not right all the time, because it's very hard.

With so many decisions to make, how can female collegiate athletes decide which path to take?

Marisa Gonzalez: You have to realize sometimes you're right and sometimes you're not. Just make sure your priorities are straight. Check your priorities. If it's family, if it's money, if it's happiness, it's not wrong whatever it is. We all have different priorities in life. They're not right or wrong, they're just yours. Work towards them. Whatever you want to do; you want to be rich, work towards that, be rich. Your actions have to go towards that goal.

I was doing events and I was good, I think. I did Pan American Games in a day. Taekwondo Championships. No idea. For people that want to get into sports in the operations side, you don't have to know every sport. I could have no idea about Taekwondo when I went in there. You have to know how to operate marketing and just do different things. You're still learning about the sport as you go. I did Pan American Games and I had rugby, water ski, mountain bike. I had no idea about those three sports.

You learn so much about each sport. Then I had the 13th Pan American Games, just for people with disabilities. I was managing all the managers. I had to learn a lot of adaptive sports, which was amazing.

It was fun. Then I had Taekwondo for two years in a row, but I did different events. I just had to learn quickly. Why? Because my priorities changed. Talking about priorities. I wanted to make a difference in people's lives and I wanted to have my sport grow. I was like, "I'm helping rugby and Taekwondo and water ski, what about women's soccer?" I wanted to get into that and wanted to coach.

I find it very rewarding, very fun, so I changed. Priorities change and just make sure what you do goes with what you want to be in life. It changes. For five years, every year I still wanted to be an architect once or twice. I think it'd be cool to be an architect or a doctor. It changes.

One thing that I thought when I was 21, 22, is that you have to pick one path and stay with that and ride that one forever. Then as I've gotten older like you said, you realize things change. I changed. My interests changed. You get exposed to something new and it makes you want to do something else. As you mentioned, you have to know that you don't know everything and that it's okay to learn something new and to mess up and change the course, as long as you're still doing something that aligns with who you are and it's part of your passion.

You make mistake with your minor or your major or sometimes you mess up on your job. You decided to change your job. You thought it was going to be better and it turns out it isn't and you're thinking, "Oh my God, I had a great thing going on there." It's ok that it changes.

Marisa, what advice, as we close, would you have for your 22-year-old self? If you could talk to her, what would you tell her?

Marisa Gonzalez: What would I tell? Oh my God, this is a good question. It's a good question though. What would I tell myself? I would just say be happy. Don't worry too much. I realized a lot of things I worried when I was in college or in high school, they have no importance in life.

Just be happy. Don't create the drama, just don't worry so much. You're in college, you skip a class and you think you're going to die. You realize, "Oh my God, I could've skipped 10 or 20." Don't do it if you're in college, but you know what I mean.

What are the final pieces of advice you would like to share with current female student-athletes?

Marisa Gonzalez: Don't worry about the little things that don't matter. Just enjoy your time, especially if you're playing sports. Enjoy, every single part of it. Enjoy the drills, the sprints, the 6:00am practices, which you probably hate.

Just enjoy that whole thing, because it's over after college. If you're lucky enough to go pro, you'll continue to enjoy it, but for most people, it's over. Just be happy with your choices and don't be so critical of yourself and others. Don't be so critical.

Marisa Gonzalez's contact information:
Email: migonzalezom@gmail.com
Facebook: Marisa Gonzalez
LinkedIn: https://linkedin.com/in/maria-gonzalez

Chapter 6: ALICIA HERALD

Current occupation: Founder of MyEdMatch.

Where did you attend college and what sport did you play?

Alicia Herald: I played basketball at Washington University in St. Louis.

How does myEDmatch work to help educators have great experiences?

Alicia Herald: That goes back to my experience directly in the classroom. I wasn't out there just trying to start a company for the sake of starting a company. For me, it was the fact that we know, after decades and decades of research, that the number one most important thing you can give kids toward leveling the playing field is education, and the number one driver is the quality of a teacher. I absolutely have the utmost respect for teachers and I think we need to continue to elevate the profession so that the best folks out there go on to teach our next generation of leaders.

When you actually look at teachers, the process for which we place them is actually pretty crazy and old school. Actually, when you look at a job posting, they all look very similar. Someone sitting in a central office oftentimes slaps you in a school.

The principal doesn't know who's coming in. There's just this old archaic system of placing teachers, and so I thought, "How could we use technology to enhance this and actually figure out where a teacher would be best aligned?" Using concepts similar to online dating, actually, is how we came up with the idea to match teachers to school based on a wide net of vision values and culture so they're a good fit there so they stay there for longer.

How did you become so passionate about this topic?

Alicia Herald: I became passionate from my own time in the classroom. I joined Teach For America and I was placed in South Central LA. Teaching in LA I saw the impact that teachers could have on kids and I knew we needed more great teachers to not only go into the profession but to stay in the profession. The more I started digging into this, my roles changed and I was the executive director of Teach For America in Kansas City where I placed teachers across there. I was looking at the data to figure out why teachers were leaving.

Seventy percent of teachers that leave every year attribute it to one of two reasons. The top one is the lack of alignment with school leaders. The people in my building, I didn't fundamentally agree on things with them. You're a free agent. You can go where you want to go, and so teachers are doing that and they're leaving schools.

Then the second piece is just transparency of workplace conditions. The want to know: "what is it going to be like when I work there?" Don't tell me it's one thing and then, in reality, it's something else. What we've actually seen is that teachers are willing to work in what some would consider the hardest schools if it's a great fit, and they'll have an awesome opportunity to grow there. My entire passion behind this is because I believe we need more great teachers staying in classrooms and teaching the kids that need it the most a lot longer in their profession.

How important is it for teachers to stay and get settled as opposed to having to change constantly?

Alicia Herald: If they are happy, they're not going to change. If not, they'll eventually just walk out of the profession. That's what we're seeing. In the news today, there's a lot about a teacher shortage. Forty-nine of our fifty states have declared that they have shortages in at least one critical area. We need more people to go into it, but we also need to treat teachers better along the way.

When you were in college, could you foresee that you'd be doing what you're doing now? When you were in undergrad?

Alicia Herald: No. Not at all. I would say the one thing that helped me was just this thirst to learn more. You would look at my transcript record, and yes, I had all my required courses for my majors, but then I was taking something just because I thought it was interesting, and so I had all these bits and pieces.

I knew that I would always do something that continued to push me to learn more. Did I think it would be in education? Not exactly, but once my eyes were open to the actual opportunity gap that kids across the country have, I figured I could play a direct role in that. I knew there was no better cause and no better thing that I wanted to fight for than educational opportunity.

Will you talk a little bit about your career progression? What was your major in undergrad? Also, did you go immediately to Teach For America or did you do some other things in between?

Alicia Herald: Yeah. I don't use a whole lot of what I went to school for, but I think that might be the case with several folks. I studied political science, Spanish, and legal studies. I had actually applied to law school as a junior in college. I graduated a little bit early. I had applied to law school and deferred my seat in law school. I was going to go into corporate law, of all things, and then join Teach For America straight out of college.

That idea was this two-year opportunity, go back, contribute in a meaningful way as a leader in education. Then right at that time, when I was teaching out in California, the budget crisis started. If you didn't have five years of teaching tenure, you literally got a pink slip, even if you were doing a great job.

I couldn't stay in teaching out in LA with my kids anymore, but I knew I wanted to remain involved in education, so I joined the staff at Teach for America. I was a traveling national recruiter. I spent all day every day on a college campus somewhere trying to convince folks that they, too, should join the fight for educational equity.

After some time recruiting teachers, I moved back to my hometown of Kansas City to open up the regional office. I grew that nonprofit arm of Teach for America in Kansas City for five years before taking the leap to start a company of all things.

Why Teach For America? Will you explain a little bit about Teach for America? There may be some young ones reading who don't know.

Alicia Herald: Yep. Teach for America is a national nonprofit whose sole purpose is to convince folks that educational opportunity is the number one cause of our generation. TFA is there to level the playing field and to close the opportunity gap for low-income kids who predominantly are kids of color across the country.

You commit to two years, you're actually a teacher, and by the end of that time, you're a certified teacher where you can stay in the profession long term.

Why did you decide to defer law school for Teach for America? You said that you wanted to give back and do some good, but you could've gone to the Peace Corps, you could've taken fellowship programs. There are tons of things you could have done. Why TFA?

Alicia Herald: For me, it was actually reflecting back on my own educational opportunities. I went to private school growing up. There were only ten kids in my class from Kindergarten through eighth grade. Then I went to a private high school and then I went to Wash U.

I literally had the best of the best when it came to educational opportunities, and I was reflecting on that and thinking, "Did all of my friends have that chance?"

I also played AAU ball growing up, and in Kansas City, we have this thing called "The Kansas City Star Scholar-Athlete" where in the newspaper they pick one high school student from every graduating class who was an academic all-star. They were upheld as not just a great athlete, but they had focused on their academics. One of my friends who I played AAU ball with and grew up with was named the scholar athlete for her school which was one of the prep schools in a public school district.

Here we are thinking, "Oh, we're going to go to this fancy dinner together and this will be so fun." She couldn't actually pass the SAT or the ACT with a high enough score to take her full-ride D1 scholarship, and here's a woman who's being upheld by her school as having done everything right, but she couldn't pass the tests. She didn't have the academic muscle that she needed to go and take this full-ride opportunity that would have changed her life, so she went to a junior college and within the first semester was pregnant and had dropped out.

When I think about her life path versus mine, it wasn't because I was better. I definitely was not better at basketball than her, and I wasn't better at academics. I had just been given a different set of opportunities. Until all kids have access to a great free public education, this is the work that I'll find myself in.

It's a shame that in this country you could almost take someone's zip code and you could predict the graduation rate from high school of a senior class of kids. Just by the zip code alone. I think that's just a huge issue and it's pervasive across the country.

What are some challenges that you face doing your work?

Alicia Herald: There are systematic things that I think we need to change about education, but then there are so many day-to-day challenges. When people ask me now, "Running and owning a tech company, what's been the greatest professional challenge of your life?" I said it was teaching nine and ten-year-olds because I don't pay them, right? They're not on my payroll, so I can't say, "I demand this of you." I think so much of what I learned about leadership I learned in the classroom.

It's this idea of "These little people are only going to listen to you if you can set a compelling vision of "Why am I going to pay attention? Why am I working so hard for you?" You need that huge goal for them to reach towards, have a vision for them. You have to invest them around it. I think you use a lot of data as a teacher in figuring out where to pivot, what changes to adapt to. I think you have to be really compelling for whatever age group of kids you have.

I'd say by far this idea of setting this big bold vision for people to rally behind and invest in kids day after day was the toughest leadership experience I had. Nevertheless, just systematically, across the country, we have a long way to go in education. It's not just education. I would say that the number one thing that we need to do is provide equal access for all kids, but we just need to respect teachers more.

When you look at other countries that are out-performing us, they are taking their best and their brightest and they are pushing them into the field of education and they're paying them well. We're not paying them near what we need to. We're not respecting the profession. I'd say that those are some of the big things when it comes to challenges that we currently have and then challenges day-to-day in the classroom.

As a leader whose goal is to inspire people and to work towards a vision and to create equity, how do you use what you've learned playing sports in your day-to-day?

Alicia Herald: I think there're so many parallels between what I do and playing sports. Even when you're on the team, I think the role of captain is interesting because it's not always the person whose name is "The Captain" that shows up as the real leader on the court. I think about the skill sets that you have and that you use when you're on the court with your teammates that you lead by example. You know you're always hustling. They're putting in the extra effort. Those same things that you learned as an athlete are transferable directly into leadership.

Whether or not we're able to accurately communicate, that is going to be the gap because you have the leadership you need. Whether or not you were the captain, whether or not your team won, whether or not you're an all-American, you were part of a team environment. You know how to get along well with others. You know that that's not always an easy road. You've learned what it means to be disciplined. You have to be organized. All of those things are what's needed in the workforce. I think that being able to take that experience and translate it effectively is really key.

I would also just say persistence. That is something that I look for so much in the people I hire today. It's "How do you respond in the face of challenges?" We all look pretty good when things are going rosy, right? When the path is clear, everyone is at their best, but I want to know who do I want in my bunker with me when things get rough, and so I ask a ton of questions about "Define a challenge for me? How did you respond? What was your initial reaction? Then after you had stepped back, what was your plan of attack to actually get over this?"

I think you can learn so much about someone from how they face adversity, and as an athlete, you're constantly facing adversity and you're learning, one, not just that you can't give up, but two, how are you going to rally the people around you and work harder than ever? That's the mentality of people I want on my team.

Who are some of the leaders who have mentored you and shown you how to lead?

Alicia Herald: Oh, this is a good question. One, I would probably go back. I'd say the best leader that I've ever learned from is my coach in college. Coach Fahey is a remarkable woman for so many reasons. We were just celebrating an award she had won and we were reflecting on what we had actually learned from Coach.

One, she would outwork anyone, and you're probably thinking, "What do you mean outwork? You're a coach. You're not actually the one on the court hustling," but she would prepare so well. We would be the most prepared team regardless of who we were playing, and those are late-night hours that she's putting in, watching tape, making sure we knew every detail about players by the time they were going to come.

I could tell you what the tendencies were of their point guard, even though I said myself, "Well, I'm never going to have to guard her," but it was the discipline that we always came prepared. We always respected our opponents no matter what we were ranked versus them, and we came ready to play.

I would say that level of discipline is something that I try and do. When I think about translating that now, I'm going to go into my board room and I'm going to sit down in front of my board and I'm going to be the most prepared person there. My team is going to be prepared for different questions that we might get asked along the way.

I think about that, and then I also just think about the culture she was able to build. My best friends, still today, were people that I met on the court, and they were so much more than their statistic, "Kelly's the great three-point shooter. Leslie is going to be dribbling the ball." These were wonderful people and she built a family environment.

That is also a sign of true leadership that you can build a culture where people can come together, and so I think about the culture I tried to build in my classroom where it didn't matter if you were the star student or not. Similarly, it didn't matter if you're the All-American or you're the person getting the water bottle. Everyone has a role and everyone's important. I learned things about culture and family-like environment that I tried to bring into my classroom, and then I definitely try and emulate today while running a company. I'm really focused on the culture that I'm building.

As young women move in their leadership journey, what are some things they should know about creating a team?

Alicia Herald: One, I do think it is respect and know your role and that every other role is important. You're obviously not going to be coming in and being the boss of much of anything, but you still play a role and you should be valued within that company. Just as much as you're trying to find the right job, you need to figure out that you're going to play a very particular role.

The role players that I want on my team and that I hire specifically for is about their mindset. I know that might sound cheesy, but I believe I can teach anyone the skills that they need to work in my company, but I can't teach mindset.

I talk a lot about growth mindset. There's a lot of research out there, but you can't ever assume that your skill or your knowledge level is fixed. You want to continue to grow and develop that. I hire people that, "You know what? You might not have experience in it yet, but when you face other challenges where you didn't actually know the direct skill set, how did you respond in that and do you think you can learn it?" That appetite for learning that craving, knowing you're always going to continue to grow, that's what I look for.

No matter where you land, your enthusiasm and your mindset can be contagious. Not saying that we expect one person to help turn a ship if you're in a culture that's not great, but people are watching and your mindset clearly sticks out above and beyond any course you've taken, any Excel spreadsheet that you might be able to produce, and so I would say lead with your mindset and continue to grow.

What are some things that are tangible that you would say that young women need to know how to do?

Alicia Herald: Some tangible things that they need to know how to do. I'd say communication is really important. I think your ability to take in information and then synthesize it and pull out those key things. You're going to be flooded. No matter where you end up in your next step, there's going to be new things coming at you all the time. How do you digest that? How do you take that in, kind of take a step back, synthesize the overwhelming amount of information, parse it down into the most critical pieces and be able to communicate that out?

I think communication is going to be critical in several ways. One, how you communicate verbally with folks. Again, your ability to keep it succinct, focused on the important things, and the same goes as well in writing. Given the number of e-mails that I receive, I really value people that can keep it to the point and that can communicate that effectively.

You will know when you're interviewing someone who's just all over the place. They can't quite focus or they start telling this one story, but then something else over here reminded them of that and they want to go over there. Young women just really need to stay focused on clear communication.

How did you learn how to communicate effectively?

Alicia Herald: There was quite a big period of coaching where I actually got coached on that. They'd say, "You don't need to send three-page long e-mails. I'm only going to read this much. Can you actually cut this down in a tenth of what you have here? Can you bold the key pieces?" Then always ask yourself, and this is some good advice, "What do you want the person leaving this conversation walking away knowing?" You might have all the supporting evidence back here, but you're not writing a thesis anymore. You want them to know X, Y, and Z, and are you communicating that?

I'd say that's the big pieces. There will be coaching along the way, but if you can ask yourself, "What key pieces of information do I want this person walking away knowing and have I given them that?"

I think we dismiss the fact that we need coaches for our entire lives, and a lot of athletes falter when they aren't proactive in finding another coach. How did you get new coaches who weren't your basketball coaches?

Alicia Herald: Yeah. One, built in, I think you're going to have a manager, and that direct manager is going to give you probably the most consistent feedback, but I would also encourage you to find someone that's not tied to your organization or appear within the organization. Find someone else where you're getting that honest feedback that's outside of who you report to. I think that's important. I think you can also ask around. I think your coaches would probably know people to say they can continue to be a resource for you and asking those folks.

I also had peer coaches along the way, and I really valued them like I did teammates. When I went in to Teach for America and I was an executive director, I was the youngest person to have the role. I was terrified of, "Oh my gosh. I don't want to say anything. I don't want to look stupid." It was just an intimidating role to step into, so I found a friend who was also in that role and I said, "Yes, I want my boss to give me feedback, but you've been here. You've been around the table. Would you mind taking me under your wing and giving me feedback?"

Before I'd go in front of the large group and present something or prep something, I'd do it with her one on one. I would especially encourage women in the workplace to find another woman to be your advocate. Again, this might not be the person who's doing your formal evaluation and performance review as your manager, but find someone that's been in that company or in that organization or in that school for a while. Women that have moved their way up are very welcome to the idea of bringing others up with them. I think you just build those genuine relationships of, "Can I stay in touch with you more frequently? I'd love some coaching. I'd love some advice."

How do you keep moving forward even though you are scared, nervous and lack some confidence when you start something new?

Alicia Herald: I'd say every transition that I've made in my life into the classroom, into the recruitment job, into the executive director, trying to figure out how the heck to start my own company, every transition has been scary because there are just simply so many unknowns. You have to think about how you respond to that. One, I think hard work is going to help. You're going to transition into something that you aren't quite ready for, so it is that level of hard work and being willing to put in that time, but it's also just confidence in yourself. You stepped up to the line before and you've taken a shot not knowing if you were going to do it, but you go for it.

For me, I look back to when I was applying to be the executive director and I had people say, "You're way too young for this. You're not experienced enough." I heard those whisperings in my ear even after I had gotten the job, and so then it was, "I'm going to outwork you and I'm going to show you that I can do this. I'm going to because I'm younger, because I'm a woman." I felt that a lot in that role. Then transitioning to my company because no one else is doing it. No one else had started this exact thing. There was no playbook on how to do it, and so my initial instinct was to say, "I think it's a great idea and someone should do it."

It took a mentor of mine saying, "Not just someone. You should do it. Stop saying it's a great idea and someone should do it. Why not you?" Now I'm trying to change that little voice in my head of, "You don't know quite what you're doing. Are you sure this is a good step?" Instead, I ask an even better question of, "Why not me?" If you all take nothing else away from this, "Why not you? Why not this leap? Why not this big jump?" You have it within you, and with hard work and persistence, you'll get there. It might not be your first time or even your second, but if you hang with it, you'll get there.

That's a really great point because it's hard. Your pride comes in, and for people to see that you don't know something, it makes you very vulnerable.

Alicia Herald: It does, but everyone else has been there. Everyone else has been scared of their first job, has been scared of that big leap, of taking that promotion. All the people that are above you have been there before, and so I would just encourage you to remember that as they do.

How do you de-stress with all of the go hard, work hard? How do you take care of you?

Alicia Herald: Well, I will admit that I am a super nerd, and so it's planned. My de-stressing time is planned into my calendar. That doesn't mean I know what I'm going to do, but setting aside time that I know is both for me and also my stuff so that they see me relax. It isn't helpful even when you're in a leadership position to be seen as constantly on because people around you feel that they need to be, and that's not the culture you want to work in. I would make sure to hold that time and set what those priorities are.

For me, it used to be reading. I wanted to stay reading. I wanted to stay up to date, and they may have been things outside of my day-to-day work. It was de-stressing for me to read this terrible book or watch this terrible TV show that I'd be embarrassed that people knew that I watched. I held those things to be true and I wrote them down because you can say something is a priority, but if it doesn't match up to how you're spending your time, you're not holding yourself accountable to that.

I would definitely make sure that you just set your priorities. If faith and family are important, I should see that by how you're spending your time. Weekends were reserved for that. It's okay to have fun, especially when you're just transitioning.

What are the final pieces of advice you would like to share with current female student-athletes?

Alicia Herald: Ask for help earlier. This particularly hit me in my company because you want everyone to see you as self-confident, of knowing what you're doing. You're trying to balance that level of confidence in your image and your reputation, but of all things, it's normal to ask for help.

If you do it earlier, you can likely stop making mistakes. I would ask some mentors and my manager for help earlier. Also because I would spin my wheels. If I didn't know how to do it right away, I would get all frustrated and then I'd spend hours upon hours doing something when all it really took was asking someone for help. It didn't mean that I was any less capable of a woman, as a professional, as a boss, as a teacher, but just ask for help earlier.

Alicia Herald's Contact Information:
Email: alicia.herald@myedmatch.com
Facebook: Alicia Herald
Twitter: @alicaherald

Chapter 7: ANNA HUNTER

Current occupation: Accountant at Ernst and Young.

Where did you go to college and what sport did you play?

Anna Hunter: Originally, I'm from Ukraine, so the first time I came to the US, it was for school. I was 18 and I got a scholarship to play at TCU. It was a great experience. I would have done everything the same in terms of tennis. I played for four years, traveled a lot. It was awesome. I just struggled a little bit in terms of identifying my major and the direction I would like to take after finishing my tennis career. That was a challenging situation I think in the first two years in college.

What did you end up majoring in and why did you select that major?

Anna Hunter: Sure. I changed my mind a lot. In the first few years, I think I was undecided the first year and then I changed my major like six times just because I think as women athletes, we spend so much time practicing and traveling and playing and we don't necessarily have the time to experience anything else outside of sports, so I feel like I didn't really have the experience and the knowledge to chose my major but I did know that I wanted to do business. Eventually, I wanted to move to New York and work in business but there are so many different directions to take so at the end I ended up majoring in communications and taking a business minor and taking just a bunch of business classes. I had a goal of going to grad school after college, so that kind of shaped my direction but it was a difficult decision.

Okay. And what did you do in that time that you're off?

Anna Hunter: I did tennis and I was prepping for the [inaudible 00:03:32] and just I needed some time to figure it out. I did a couple of internships but I needed the time to kind of transition from playing full time to like, "what am I going to do now?"

When you went back to school, what did you get your Masters Degree in?

Anna Hunter: Accounting. I think that when I was still at TCU, I was considering doing finance but then we had the whole financial crisis that happened, so I wasn't really sure if that's the direction to take and then I was very interested in working at big four. So, at the end, I ended up going to grad school and getting my degree in accounting.

Nice. Now how did you go about securing your first job after college? What was that process like?

Anna Hunter: Hard. I think that was the hardest year because there was so much competition out there, so I did spend a lot of time just reading all the interview books and browsing the web and just reading how to interview and how to position yourself and how to present yourself in the way that you want to be perceived and presented.

Definitely a lot of research, a lot of reading. I think that's what I did in my year off. I was just prepping for the interviews after grad school.

So, after grad school, you ended up working ... You've been at EY since you left grad school. Was that your first job after?

Anna Hunter: I started out my career at Pricewaterhouse Coopers and I was there ... There, I spent about three years and then I came to EY.

Got you. How did you decide which companies you wanted to work for? A lot of young athletes are trying to ... as soon as they're in college, they're trying to figure out where to go; and how do they know what's a good fit?

Anna Hunter: Well, I'm not sure if I needed a platform so that ... All the big fours are huge firms and they give you a platform but then also, every book for it, like they're different. Pricewaterhouse is different from EY, so in terms of that, I didn't know. I went to Pricewaterhouse because I got an interview at Pricewaterhouse and they hired me but I wasn't sure the difference between Pricewaterhouse and EY at the time.

I did know that I wanted a big platform for not just like learning technical skills but also potentially getting involved in other initiatives going forward, so I started out at Pricewaterhouse just because it's big four and I wanted to learn the technical skills but I think at that time, I did not have the knowledge that I have now.

What are some challenges, maybe, that you face as you've made different career choices?

Anna Hunter: I think maybe what would be helpful as one of my biggest challenges there was a lack of mentors when I was in college. You know what I mean? I feel like as athletes, we always have coaches and maybe mentors that guide us in terms of our sports career but then, I never thought that maybe I would need a mentor in terms of helping me decide which direction I should take after school. I didn't really think about it in a way.

I did have my academic advisor who helps you chose classes, but I didn't really have the access and the networks that I have now working at EY and it's great here because I have access to all these mentors and partners, but back in college, I think I just didn't look for it. I'm sure if I knew that that's something that I would need, I would reach out, but that's something that I didn't know at that time.

What are some mistakes that you've made? What are some of the things that you can think about that could have done differently or a great lesson that you've learned?

Anna Hunter: I think that's my biggest mistake because that resulted in me taking a year off just to take the time to figure it out because I didn't have mentors. I figured it out from browsing the web and talking to people who I would teach tennis during that year and just by reading books but I didn't have mentors.

If I could go back, I would spend more time with my professors or maybe somebody I would work for during an internship. I just needed that access to mentors and even I would definitely take a more active role in terms of reaching out to people and asking for advice and help and kind of help them guide me in a way in terms of next steps just because I'd played tennis my whole life since I was seven years old. I didn't know anything else besides tennis.

Many athletes hardly have the time to get involved in other things that they can—maybe intern and work for different firms and even like little places—I didn't have that. I definitely needed some time off to figure it out.

Now that you are in the professional world and have so much to manage, how do you de-stress from work?

Anna Hunter: I think nothing special. Just taking the time to myself especially in the weekend. I try to work out because that relaxes you in a way. Even taking a few minutes to stretch helps. I'm trying to get into meditating. I'm not good at it and I definitely don't do too much but I try. It's something on my to-do list; to learn how to meditate or just to take care of everything and just sit in silence for a few minutes.

Nothing special. Just going for a walk in the evening or just taking some time to myself and we need to remember to do that because we forget and I feel like today, with all the social media and all the messages that we get on a daily basis, it's so hard to find the time to relax, so you forget very often. It's something we need to remember.

What are the most important aspects of being able to find balance in your life in such a busy world?

Anna Hunter : I think it kind of goes back to learning more about yourself and figuring out. You have to know who you are and what works for you because what works for me might not work for somebody else but definitely I think just taking the time off—either it's a vacation or just like a day off on a weekend or even an hour—and just think where am at right now. Am I stressed? Am I not? What do I need to do next?

Sometimes there is actually the workload that causes stress and then other times, it's the people who you work with that cause stress. They ask, how do you handle conflicts in the workplace? How do you deal with that to resolve those?

Anna Hunter: Well, I always try to be diplomatic. I do believe that people that I work with are aiming towards the same goal at the end and I'm not very good at it at all times but I always try to step into other people's shoes and kind of try to see where they are coming from and see their perspective. I may take some time to digest that, but if I disagree I definitely speak. In a non-aggressive way, I will say, "Okay. I disagree because of the following reasons."

I'm lucky to be working with the people that I like and I feel like a conflict is not always a negative thing. It can be a good thing because you can come up with a solution or resolution as long as you just try to understand the other person's perspective and show them where you're coming from and try to agree on a mutually beneficial solution that should work.

Being diplomatic is important, then also being able to hear the other person's side is important as well. Let's say if somebody doesn't agree with you, the first reaction could be, you get heated and you just want to say that you disagree but I always try to even take an hour to think about it or even sleep on it and maybe say, "Okay. This is what you think. Let's discuss it tomorrow," and give them time to digest it so we could talk about it the following day and usually, that would be the way to go for me. That works for me.

What are some ways that you use sport in your day-to-day life? I'm sorry. What are some ways that you use the lessons that you've learned from playing sports in your day-to-day?

Anna Hunter: Sure. Definitely bouncing back. Things don't always go the way you want them to go, so definitely the need to be resilient and just bounce back quickly and say, "Okay, that didn't go the way I wanted it to go. It's okay. Let's just move forward." I think that's strongest.

I think hard work also because we spend so much time practicing and just traveling and multitasking is a good one also. I'm not afraid to work hard and work extra hours and definitely, multitasking is something that I've learned from playing.

One of the things that we talk about often is that the skills that you learned during sport, you're able to transfer—discipline, hard work, sacrifice; a lot of those are intangible. Given the current job market What are some tangible skills that young women need to have for graduating?

Anna Hunter: Well, the job market is very competitive right now and I think two things. Confidence is something that's intangible but then also has credibility. You have to be able to back it up.]. A lot of people are graduating with the same major and this way, you have to find a way to differentiate yourself. Even on the resume. Even maybe getting involved in a couple of internships but something that would give you that credibility and show something that will show how you would differentiate and stand out from the crowd. Definitely in terms of intangible skills is you have to be confident but you will be hopefully confident if you have something to back it up. You have the credibility.

Definitely, in a way, you need to stand out and maybe specialize in something or differentiate yourself in a way—it depends on the major and the industry.

Why did you choose the accounting field?

Anna Hunter: I don't know. I like consulting. I like the idea of helping the clients. I never thought I would be an accountant but I do like the idea of consulting and helping the client and helping them resolve any kind of issues they might have. That's what drives me. Just at the end of the day saying, "I helped my clients to resolve a problem," or, "I helped with something else."

What is the typical day like for you as an accountant?

Anna Hunter: Well, since I'm in client services, I usually get in around 8:30 because I try to be here before the client gets in and it has changed a lot. When I just started out, it was a lot of technical skills so I had to do a lot of technical work and a lot of documenting and the writing and now it's more spending time going to meetings which I like more and more.

It's more like managing the team, managing people who work for you and also since it's managing in both directions at my level now, I'm managing downwards and also upwards, so definitely talking to a lot of people. A lot of talking, a lot of reading too, going to meetings and writing. Documenting a lot of emails. I think up to 300 emails a day.

It varies in terms of the hours working at big four—I would work a lot of hours, but it does vary. We have some downtime and we have busy times. The thing is, I like what I do. I like helping the clients, so my days go by very fast. I get in and then I'm like, "How is it 1:00 PM already? I feel like I just got in."

What are some of your career goals?

Anna Hunter: Well, I'm inspired by Beth Brooke-Marciniak. She is the Global VP of Public Policy at Ernst and Young and her responsibilities extend up to like over I think 150 countries and she advocates for the advancement of women. Since I'm very inspired by her. I dream big so maybe one I can get some impact to that extent or even a little bit of that would be awesome but we'll see.

I re-evaluate my goals every year. I think that's something that I also could have done back in college every year because we do change and grow and just learn. By learning new things, you can evaluate your plan. Every year, I try to set up a goal like long-term goals but then I do make a step back every once in a while and kind of re-evaluate it and a lot of them change.

The person that you were at 22 isn't necessarily the person you are at 32 or 42 and so, it's important that we continuously set new goals based on new interests because they will come.

Anna Hunter: Yeah. Maybe that was one of my other mistakes I haven't done back in college. I should have set the goals and then re-evaluated them.

What are the final pieces of advice you would like to share with current female student-athletes?

Anna Hunter: Women athletes should be involved in internships because you don't really know what you like until you try it. It all might sound great or maybe something different from great but you need to try it out. Even if it's a short internship, even a month, or even if it's unpaid. You can just reach out and ask if you can help with something in a particular profession—as long as you get a chance to experience the field and learn things. That's how you learn about what you like and what you don't like.

The other important thing is networking. I think that it's very important to network with others. Expanding your network, again reaching out to people and even going to networking events can help you.

Anna Hunter's Contact Information:

Email: annasydorska@hotmail.com

Instagram: Ania_Hunter

Chapter 8: EMILY JASKOWIAK

Current occupation: School-based speech and language pathologist.

Where did you attend college and what sport did you play?

Emily Jaskowiak: I played basketball at the University of Tulsa.

What do you consider your greatest athletic accomplishment?

Emily Jaskowiak: Well, funny enough, I think my greatest athletic accomplishment happened after the years of college basketball and high school basketball. How could there be anything else? I think ... I can't remember what year this was, in 2010 maybe, basketball was over and I started thinking, "I gotta do something active," so I started distance running.

I ran a half marathon and thought, "Wow, that was awesome," and I said to myself, "I'm going to run a full marathon." I ran a full marathon and I was like, "Whoa. This is the high you get?" The runner's high is real. That was great so I kept going and went for an ultra marathon,"which is any distance over a marathon." There was a 50 miles race that I found out about, and I decided to run that race! I did, and I completed it.

That's my greatest accomplishment, because of the inexperience. I went from half marathon to ultra marathon probably within two years. I've learned so many lessons from these long training runs, such as just stick with it. I had to get up early and do two runs a day, just like you remember two practices a day. I would be doing two a day to try to get all my miles in for the week. The commitment I made to do that race was pretty massive.

What was one of your most challenging races?

Emily Jaskowiak: Specifically, I had one training run that was a 40-mile training run. I was on mile 10, and I just had this breakdown, and was thinking, "I can't do it." He's my husband now, but at that time, we were not married, and he did all of my training runs with me. I just sat on this bench, just crying, feeling like, "I can't do it. I just can't. This is too hard. I'm going to get injured." At times, all the fears just come crashing down on you.

I just sat on that bench and cried for a little while. Then, I got up, and then my husband sat with me and was said, "You're going to be fine. You can do this," so he gave me time. I got up, ran 30 more miles, and was done with that training run. That kind of instances happen all the time, I've learned. I have the language and perspective now because sometimes you think the world will come crashing in, and you'll feel like you can't do it, but then you get up and you do it.

That was a really hard race, and I did it. I have not done anything like that since, but I think that was quite an accomplishment for me, especially from a basketball perspective where running is your punishment. I had to shift my mindset from considering running a punishment to thinking, "Man, this is really an enjoyable thing for me."

Why did you select running out of all the things you could've done— kickboxing, Zumba?

Emily Jaskowiak: That's a good question. I was in a previous marriage that was not great, and so it was a rough and stressful time. Running was a way for me to de-escalate and get my thoughts together, and get some alone time, and be healthy for a while. I did a lot of running, and I did a lot of thinking. I wasn't with anybody else. It was something I could plan, and do, and go at my own pace, and not have anyone else trying to pull my strings. I think that's part of it.

Going back to when you were in college. What did you major in, and why did you select your major?

Emily Jaskowiak: I was a mess. I went into college thinking I'm going to be an art teacher, so somewhere in education, I took art classes and I kind of was an art major, and I was thinking, "Oh, this is going to be great." Then I decided, I didn't want to do art. That was not the challenge I want in life.

I went round, and round, and I went to our college and career center. If people hadn't gone to those places, they should go, because I took a bunch of tests, and I talked to a counselor. Eventually, at the top of my list, at every single test I took, and every single interview thing I did, it was speech and language pathologist, but I didn't want to be a speech and language pathologist because my aunt was a speech and language pathologist. I didn't want to just follow the status quo, but they said, "Well, at least take a class," and I agreed.

Once I took the class, I knew I would be a speech and language pathologist. I really like science, not math so much, but I really like science, and I really like people. It's a great mix of science and working with people. That's what really drew my love for it. I went to that one class, it was like Intro to Speech and Language Pathology, and stuck with it.

It's important that student-athletes utilize the resources that are on campus. Why do you think student athletes often underutilize this resource?

Emily Jaskowiak: Mainly because your downtime in college is so precious. When you're not studying, and you're not at practice, and you're not doing other things required by the team, you have downtime. Many athletes simply want to sit and do whatever they want. They don't want to go and make an appointment somewhere. They don't want to be committed to something else.

They just want to have a time for themselves. That was something that a lot of people were decided, "No, we have this day off. I am not doing that." My perspective was, "Well I'm lost, so I'm going," and I'm really glad I did. Sometimes they miss out on people and resources that can help them. I know that I was one of the very few people that went.

How did you go about securing your first job?

Emily Jaskowiak: Well, I'm in a really fortunate position, because speech and language pathologists are in very high demand. I think it depends on the region of the United States you live in, but I would say in most regions there's a need. The acronym for speech and language pathologists is SLP. There is an SLP shortage.

With a speech and language pathology degree, you're trained from communication disorders from birth to death. You can work in a school, you can work in a nursing home, you can work in a hospital, you can work in a long-term care facility, you can work in a private setting. There's a trillion options for you. I knew I wanted to work in a school, and so I just put my application out there to a bunch of schools in my area, and I think I got job offers for almost all of them, and I just picked the one I wanted and started working.

Did you have any other degrees before entering the workforce?

Emily Jaskowiak: I played five years, I redshirted my freshman year. I got that first year of grad school paid for with my scholarship, which was great. This is one of those hindsight things, like how incredible a scholarship is. You don't really know it at the time, but now I do. I just had one year, I had to go to school for six years. A two-year master program. I had to pay for that one last year, which my parents ended up helping me after my divorce.

I went six years, and I graduated in May of 2007 with a master's. I think I was probably hired for a job before I even graduated. That's kind of how it is right now for SLP's. You're in demand.

Young athletes contact me because my school district has openings, so let them know where you are. I now live in Kelso, Washington, which is about 40 miles north of Portland, Oregon. All up in the northwest, we could use some SLP's, so move out here, it's gorgeous!

Talk about the move. Your career progression, you were in Tulsa for awhile, in Oklahoma, but you made the decision to relocate. Why'd you make that decision?

Emily Jaskowiak: Well, after I was in this marriage and got a divorce, things really changed for me. It was never diagnosed, but I know I battled with some depression along with that. Again, running was one of those things that helped me kind of work out of that.

When you're doing sports your whole life, and you're dedicated, it is so much of your life; you don't have time for much else. When I got done with sports, I ran, and I started getting involved with outdoor activities such as camping, and backpacking, and hiking, and trail running. I realized that trail running is awesome. There's not a whole lot of opportunity for that in Oklahoma though.

Again, he's my husband now, but at the time we were just dating, we would be driving for the weekend four hours to get to some places to camp. Eventually, we were like, "You know, we should just move somewhere that better suits what we want to do in life." We took a few trips. We visited Colorado, we visited New Mexico, we visited Portland. We know we didn't want east coast because Brian moved from the east coast, so we wanted something different.

We just fell in love with the Portland area, and so I applied for jobs. Guess what? SLP's are in need, so I got hired and we moved out. Brian did not have a job at the time, he got hired later. He's also an educator. Yeah, it was a pretty big leap of faith, and it's a big risk, but it was well worth it because this is a great place for us. We do all kinds of camping, and hiking, and backpacking, and stuff.

How does your athletic background impact your professional life?

Emily Jaskowiak: I think a lot of athletes will identify with being really competitive. I know a personality trait of mine is being an achiever, and maybe sometimes an overachiever. There are opportunities in work all the time to advance, get more money, and be higher up. For me, that would be a special education director or a principal. However, about six years ago maybe, I had to really back down and really think about it what I wanted.

If I wanted more money, more status, and to be this achiever in my field, I would have to give up all these other things that I wanted to do in life. For my husband and I, we both live with the mind frame that we work so we can live and do what we want to do, and not the other way around.

That's been a challenge for me to say no to some things, and decide, "No, I don't want a year-round job, because I wouldn't have this time in the summer to spend with my family, and go camping, and do all these things I want to do." That's a tough choice every time because I want to be that overachiever, you know?

What are some of the challenges you faced as you've made different career choices?

Emily Jaskowiak: Lots of challenges. Challenges are at every corner. Like the challenge of choosing what you want to do—that was a challenge. Then, getting involved but not getting overly competitive or overly achieving is a lot for me. The students that I work with, they're students with disabilities who need a lot of help. I want to give way more than I can, and then I carry that home. Then, I feel guilty. I'm stressed about it at times because I never feel like helping enough. Often times I lose sleep over it. I know a lot of people in special education have this same kind of feelings.

It's constantly a challenge for me to break up my school, professional life, and my home life. It's always a juggling act, always. You can use that analogy in almost every aspect of life, but it's just another one of those big juggling acts when you think, "I've got to create some balance here, and find balance," and that's always a challenge. Now that I've added a pretty rigorous school to it—with getting this doctorate degree—I've added a third ball to the mix, and it's just made that juggling challenge a lot more difficult.

What's a mistake that you've made and how did you bounce back from it?

Emily Jaskowiak: A mistake? There're so many mistakes. I would say daily mistakes. I'll try to pick one because I feel like my first marriage was kind of a big mistake. I came back from that with a lot of support from people, and a lot of running.

On a different note, I know I make parenting mistakes all the time. I have two little children, one and four years old and that's kind of like a blind test. You don't know what to expect, and you don't know what to do and what you're doing.

I make mistakes all the time, and I think the way I overcome it is to not feel guilty about it. I recognize it was a mistake, admit it. That's usually big. People that can't admit mistakes are not going to grow. I say to myself, "Yeah, I did that wrong, but I'm going to do it differently next time, and just keep your eyes and mind frame looking forward, and not dwelling on the mistake.

I also make tons of mistakes in my career. It's a lot of judgement calls for me when I'm testing a student or making a diagnosis. Sometimes I'm not really sure if this is the right way to go, but to the best of my ability, this is what I think I should do at this time. I go with it. I realize often this was not the right choice. When you realize you made a mistake, you switch it, and you move on. Don't dwell on it, just admit your mistake, and constantly think about what you're going to do differently. After a while doing it differently, mistakes don't become that big of a deal.

How do you bounce back after you've made a mistake?

Emily Jaskowiak: I use humor to make fun of myself a lot, and to point out things that I do that I know other people relate to, but maybe would not admit to. Hey, we're all human here. When I make a giant, hilarious mistake, and I'm going to laugh. I'm going to choose to think this is funny, and that's going to help me move on, rather than feeling sad, or disappointed, or frustrated.

There's a slew of other emotions you could feel that will make you feel bad, but I'm not going to feel bad about this. I'm just going to keep on rolling with it.

Also, I use humor to diffuse a lot of stressful situations. If someone's being uptight at work, I'm going to lighten up that situation real quick and so we can move on because we cannot be sitting in a funk. For me, we're moving on.

What are some of the transferable skills that you've had playing sports that you use in your day-to-day, in addition to being competitive?

Emily Jaskowiak: That's pretty easy. From the time I was really young, I realized that almost everything I'm doing in life I've learned from sports or having pets and animals. There's a lot of responsibility with that. I think the biggest thing that is transferable, and people tell me this—they notice it and tell me—is to know how to be a part of a team.

I need people to realize that being part of a team is far beyond being on a sports team, or being on whatever kind of traditional team you might be thinking. Being on a team really breaks down to how well you work with people. There's nothing you're going to do in life that you don't have to work with people. Just understanding the dynamics of how a team works.

As a member of a team, you should always be focused on the bigger picture and the bigger goal. I do that pretty easily and I know other people have a harder time with it. That's worked well for me. Just being able to work with people or maybe even your family. This definitely spills over into relationships.

You recognize who's a good teammate, and who's not a good teammate. You want to surround yourself with a good team. There're so many analogies and metaphors. I say it all the time, I'm not going to surround myself with a bad team. If you are going to be a bad teammate, then I'm not going to put any energy towards you.

I think my husband is a really great teammate, because there's a team dynamic there where you're only as strong as your weakest link, right, so we better both be pretty freaking strong.

At work, just working with teachers, and people, and knowing when you need to be a captain on your team, versus when you need to be a player on the team. It's just all dynamics that you learn from being on a team. That goes in so many places.

Would you give an example of when you knew you should've been the captain of the team, or when you have to step back and let someone else lead?

Emily Jaskowiak: There are lots of instances. An area where I've had to step up recently was with a student that I'm working with. I'm not the person in charge of this student's file or this student's education plan, but I'm a part of the team. However, for this scenario, some people were dropping the ball. I knew I had the knowledge to lead this team, so I kind of just took it over, and got some things rolling.

That's one example of where I was like, "You know this is recognizing the situation that was going on," and saying, "Oh, I need to take hold of this and move forward, and kind of guide the rest of these people to where we need to be going with this kid."

Another example of where I did not have to be the leader was, I work with a team of speech pathologists in my district, there's seven of us, and everybody is good in their own right. Actually, a plan that we're doing for next year is we're going to redefine some roles, because I'm new to the team, and I'm recognizing there really aren't any roles, and you can't have seven captains. You've got to have some sort of leadership.

We were planning this big event, and this girl, she's a very good friend of mine, but she's also a young new speech path, and she kind of headed stuff up, and I'm like, "All right, well I need to be there to guide her and help her," but I really didn't. She had it. I just kind of fell back into more of a player role and let her do her thing. She totally succeeded and flew with it. I think it was a great experience for our whole team. Those are some examples.

One of the things I hear quite often is we know that the skills we learn through playing sports transfers throughout our life, but some of the young women coming out haven't necessarily had the experience yet to see the application of those things that we learn from playing sports. How do those skills apply?

Emily Jaskowiak: Yeah. It applies to everything. It might be a jump or a transition to see how that applies to everything, but players would benefit from using some positive self-talk such as "You've got this. You've done this before. If you think about it, you've been in this situation before, and it was probably a lot harder. You got this." I have to do that all the time.

What was your experience when you first started playing sports competitively?

Emily Jaskowiak: I think I was in 4th grade, so all I did was sprint from one end of the court, to my spot, to the other end of the court, to my spot. I was like, "Yes, I'm good." I didn't even know there was so much more that I had to learn. Once I started, I learned to be patient.

You're used to being up there, and the leader, and you have to go through that learning process over and over where you are not good, and be patient with yourself, and use some self-talk, and say, "You know what? You are going to be fine. Just keep at it, you're going to be fine. Wake up the next morning, and it's going to be fine. The sun will set, and the sun will rise, and you'll get there."

What are the final pieces of advice you would like to share with current female student-athletes?

Emily Jaskowiak: You are just going to be wonderful. That's going to be my advice because there are things that you don't even know, that you have learned, and you're going to figure that out. It's been 10 years for me since I've hung up the college basketball shoes. Actually, I think I threw them in the trash. I know, as an athlete, maybe you get sick of it. I was kind of ready to be done, and I had some hurtful coaches, and learning how to rebound from that was one thing. Just know that you've done a lot, and you've got a great foundation.

Something else I had been thinking about, because I hear this phrase all the time, is "Well, that chapter of my life is done." It is part of your story, but I don't think it's ever gone. It's part of your story, and it's going to be a constant thread running through your life at all times. You can't separate yourself from what you've learned.

It's in your book, and there are going to be portions of that in every single chapter from now on. It's not like you're not going to use that stuff. Yes, you may be finished with the competitive playing, but it's going to be written in the rest of the chapters in your life.

It might be hard if you're ending your career right now to think what a blessing it was, but it really was. It might take you a couple of years to come roundabout, to realize that, because maybe you're bitter, I don't know, but it was a good thing. It was a good thing.

Some college athletes feel like they have died when their career's over. You're getting a least on a whole new life, and you've got all of these skills. Go and run with it. That was literally for me, and I ran. The world is your oyster, so go and live it!

Emily Jaskowiak's Contact Information:
Email: emily.jaskowiak@gmail.com
Facebook: Emily Jaskowiak

Chapter 9: JOI MADISON

Current occupation: Owner of EAT.SLEEP.SWEAT. Functional Fitness.

Where did you attend college and what sport did you play?

Joi Madison: Yeah. I went to California State University of Northridge, or CSUN, out in Northridge, California, and I played water polo there.

How did you start playing water polo?

Joi Madison: Oh, very, very interesting. I grew up as a swimmer in L.A. I actually did not play water polo until I got to college. Long story short, I had just moved back from New York, where I was potentially going to go to Hofstra University and play volleyball. That didn't work out for a number of different reasons, and I came back.

A friend of mine who I used to swim with was swimming at Northridge. As a result of Title IX and all the things that were going on with Title IX, equal funding for women in sports became available. They were starting a women's water polo team at Cal State, Northridge. They were looking for girls. I had swim experience, and so he said, "Hey, I talked to the coach. She's interested." I spoke to her, and that was really my first run at water polo. I actually ended up going to school for water polo, a sport that I had never played prior to that. But as a strong swimmer and an athlete, I did what I had to do to pick it up and be successful.

You took on a new challenge and got it done?

Joi Madison: Yeah. Absolutely. They were talking about free schooling, and I was like, "Look, you figure it out. It's a ball. How bad could it be?" You know?

What was your greatest accomplishment in your athletic career?

Joi Madison: I was an All-American swimmer. In my freshman year, I made the All-American swimming team for the 50-meter breaststroke event. That was pretty cool. You know, waking up early and being in the pool at 5:00 a.m. Then, for somebody to recognize it and say, "Hey, your competitive nature and your success in the sport has landed you recognition nationwide." I would say that that's probably one of the highlights of my career as an athlete.

What was your major and why did you select that major?

Joi Madison: Ultimately, I got my bachelor's in Kinesiology with an emphasis in exercise science. Also, pretty interesting story, I started off as a dance major. I'm really tall. I'm about 6'2, 6'3. My mom knew that I was going to be tall, and so she started putting me in dance classes when I was very young so that I would be graceful and coordinated. Anyway, I grew up. I loved to dance. My freshman year I thought, "I'll be a dance major." Then, it was kind of like, "Well, I'm not going to be a professional dancer. I don't really want to be a dance teacher."

I moved through a range of different majors. I went, then, to physical education. At the time, they were slashing jobs, budgets were being cut, and P.E. jobs were being cut. I thought, "I'm going to graduate and not have a job."

Then, I moved through a couple of different things. Ultimately, I landed in kinesiology. I did physical therapy and I did athletic training. I tried all these different hats on under the kinesiology umbrella, and I landed at exercise science. It was the bio-mechanics of understanding movement. That was what really grabbed my attention. It stuck.

I think it was great for me that I bounced around then when I still had the comfort of being in school and having that cushion. I ended up doing kinesiology exercise science. That's what I graduated in, and I love it. I had a great time.

You know, you bring up something that's pretty common. Most people, athlete or not, bounces around from different major to major. It helps you really figure out your niche. Why is it important for student-athletes to explore various majors?

Joi Madison: I think a large part of the college experience is just that—the experience. Of course, the knowledge that you get and the education is important, but actually being able to explore and experience different things within that environment of having that safety and that cushion of not being out in the "real world" while you're figuring it out is, actually, really cool. For me, because I'm in the same general area, now with my trainer and the company, and with my clients, I get to pull from all of that.

I get to be creative like I was in dance, and I get to help my clients in the healing process because I have an education in the physical therapy realm, or athletic training with taping and proper stretching techniques. I get to pull from all of that experience, and that helps me separate and differentiate myself as a trainer because I have all of these different influences that impact my style of training. It didn't go to waste at all.

How did you go about securing your first job after you finished playing? What was that process like?

Joi Madison: While I was in college, I was lifeguarding and I was coaching a junior national water polo team. When I graduated, I stuck with doing that for a while. I actually fought doing personal training. I valued what I'd learned and what I knew so much that I didn't want to be lumped in with people who took a little course for six weeks and said, "Oh, I'm a trainer." Not that there's anything wrong with that. I certainly did become certified in that area, as well, with a couple of different national associations.

I felt like I had a much deeper understanding of the body and human movement and sports, as an athlete and as a coach, and from all these different perspectives and angles. I was just like, "I don't want to be lumped in with people who took a class, and now we're making the same amount of money." I felt like I was owed something more.

I always knew I wanted to have my own space. I started looking for a job, but I looked specifically for a job where I could have a contact and connection with the owners so that as I'm getting experience as a trainer, I can also get insight as a business owner of what that looks like, what the process is and what mistakes did they make. They were incredibly helpful with giving me some of the books that they read and all of that. I actually found my first job on Craigslist, believe it or not. I looked in the Craigslist directory, and I found this job. It was great because it was a privately owned facility. They had a very limited membership. I knew that it was a great place for me to learn a lot about the business and not just be working as a trainer.

The place where my studio is in, I actually found that on Craigslist as well. Craigslist has been a huge resource for me in my professional career. Never discount those simple spaces. You never know where you're going to find a gym.

What has been your career progression? First, your job after college, you worked in a studio. Then, what happened after that?

Joi Madison: Like I said, I always knew I wanted to have my own facility, so I went in with that as my foundation, in terms of every move that I made, wanting to get closer to that. I went in. I gave myself a couple of years to learn.

I think I did about two to two-and-a-half years at that studio. Eventually, I branched out and started working as an independent contractor. I started renting space at another studio. Fortunately, because of relationships that I had formed and the work that I had done, a couple of my clients, when I left that facility, they followed and came with me. So, I had a small client base at that time.

Then, what I also started doing was I worked for the city of Los Angeles. I started working for the Department of Recreation and Parks. I started a program for teens where I built the fitness curriculum for the teenagers, who were members of the particular facility, with the expo center down near USC. With my personal training, I also started to implement what I learned as a P.E. major with building curriculum. That also helped me form a reputation in the community with people, working with athletes, and doing things like that.

Ultimately, as an independent contractor, I started building my clientele, my reputation. I started really cementing my training philosophy and style. Then, word of mouth. Ultimately, the opportunity arose when I found my space on Craigslist, and I just jumped on it. It's really been unconventional, in a lot of ways. I didn't do a whole lot of business planning and taking classes and learning. I really skipped over a lot of that.

I'm approaching my two-year anniversary next month of owning the studio, and I'm just now getting to that part. Usually, people do that first and then they move into the business. I found the brick and mortar, and was like, "Ready, set, go."

I dove right in, which tends to be my style in a lot of things. You heard the story about diving right into water polo. Literally, diving right into it.

My progression has just always been to keep in mind my purpose, making sure every decision I make and every step that I take is moving me closer to that. Even if it doesn't feel like I'm ready, on some level. I was not, at all, ready to own my own studio. But the opportunity presented itself, and so, I said, "You know what? If not now, when?" I know myself well enough to know that if I'm in it, I'm going to do what it takes to stay. And that's what it's been so far.

What are some challenges that you faced going through this entire process of owning your own company and just diving in?

Joi Madison: Oh, gosh. How long do you have? What I should also say, for a number of reasons, is I've done this whole process cash-out-of-pocket. I didn't get any loans. I don't have any investors. This has really been, in the truest essence of the words, a solo project. I think the challenge has been allowing myself breathing room.

I think athletes will be able to relate from the perspective of being very competitive and sometimes being critical of ourselves. We look at playback of games or we think of the game. We're like, "I should have, I could have, we could have," or whatever. We don't often allow ourselves a lot of room for error because sometimes error means win or lose, and that could be championship situation. There are different scenarios.

I think my biggest challenge has been to step back and see, this is—if we're looking from the athlete's perspective—where my teammate comes in. Maybe I'm not a great shooter or maybe I'm not a great defensive player. Here's where my teammate steps in. Marketing is not why I got into business, so I need to be okay with relinquishing control of that and giving it to someone else.

Not feeling like the burden is on me because of whatever reason. For me, it's been less about the actual process of doing the business and more about my approach to the process of doing the business. And really allowing myself the room to have teammates and let my teammates do their job.

Swimming is an individual sport. I'm in my lane. This is my race. It's not about you. I've had to adjust my mind to more of a team sport approach, if you will.

Being willing to let go and let teammates carry is hard when you're used to your individual performance being able to determine much of the outcome. How did you decide that? Why did you decide to relinquish?

Joi Madison: I understood that the purpose and the reason that I'm doing what I do is so much greater than me. The same reason why I agreed to contribute to this project is because I understand it's so much bigger than me. If I get caught up in trying to do it all, I know that something's going to suffer. It won't be to the full capacity and potential of what it could be in terms of the impact and the people that I can reach.

I think, for me, it was just saying, "Hey! It's time for you to remember why you started and let that be your focus. Then, these other things that are essential and important, but not necessarily your strong suit, that's where you call in your teammates." I was really just about understanding that if I really want to go for the impact that I know I'm supposed to make, I have to allow somebody to help me. Otherwise, I'm sacrificing what this is supposed to be.

How do you de-stress from everything?

Joi Madison: Particularly, as a business owner, even though I have relinquished control in some areas, I still do wear a lot of hats. What's important for me to do is always factor into my schedule, physically on my calendar, time where I'm not working. Occasionally, I might have to schedule a meeting somewhere in between there. That happens, but for the most part, I try to keep that block of times, maybe a couple of hours in the day, just completely clean. That could be for a nap. That could be for my own workout. It's hard for me to squeeze them in because I'm always doing someone else. That could be for prayer or meditation, which I do a lot. Or journaling. Typically, I have my quiet time during that time.

I really prioritize that because a lot of times, especially with working out, the number one thing I hear from people is, "I don't have time" So, I make time for myself. Every day, on my calendar, when I'm scheduling my clients, I say, "I'm not taking anybody during this block of time." That's how I allow myself to have what I call a white noise downtime, quiet time, or just whatever I choose to do. And that's for me. No one gets to infringe on that.

There are a number of clichés the encourage people to never take a break and keep pushing. As a professional in the industry, how do you feel about this mindset?

Joi Madison: Oh, gosh. I hate it. I know from an experiential standpoint of having been sleep deprived, and also from the knowledge of what sleep deprivation does to your body. The pressure that you hear from a coach that says, "You sleep when you're dead," or, "Grinding all night. You sleep we grind," all these things that people say.

You start to feel pressure. "Could I be further along in my business if I would be willing to sacrifice this?" I'm going to bed at 10:30 feeling guilty because I know somebody's up until 4:00 in the morning. I'm like, "Oh!"

You know, "And then what?" I want to do this because I know the value of it. I don't want to create an environment where I begin to resent it. Then, I'm no longer excited about doing work that is so relevant and so important. I don't want to create that kind of environment around what I'm called to do, so I just keep that in perspective. I prioritize myself because I know, maybe for a week or two, it is non-stop.

You have seasons where you do have to grind, and you do have to burn the midnight oil. I get that, but long term chronically, it's not worth it. No matter how much you love what you do, you can't do it without your health. If you're not sleeping well and taking the time to prioritize yourself in some way, you are sabotaging and putting your health at risk. It's not worth it.

You are absolutely right. What are your long term goals? What's your vision?

Joi Madison: I called it Eat.Sleep.Sweat. because I started doing miniature blogs. This was back when Facebook had notes. I was making notes and sharing fitness information with my friends. I would sign off, and I would say, "Eat, sleep, sweat." That was my sign off.

When it started to come into more of a clear view for me that I was getting closer to having my own, I started playing with the idea of names. It came up, and I said, "I really like it." It's comprehensive. It deals with the nutrition. It deals with the rest and recovery. It deals with the fitness. It deals with all of that. I think that we need to have a much more comprehensive and holistic approach to fitness. It can't just be about one thing.

One of the things I say to my clients all the time is that you cannot compartmentalize your life. My vision for Eat.Sleep.Sweat. moving forward is that we will be the premier place to come and get all things health and wellness, from emotional and spiritual wellness to mental health to your physical health with working out and fitness.

I'll be starting school in the fall. I'm going back. I'm going to get a master's in clinical psychology. That is because I want to be well-equipped to help people deal with the mental aspect of their fitness and health journey. I really want to be that premier location. I want to help people connect the dots.

We want to be able to explore things such as, What's going on in your social-cultural environment? How is that impacting your health and the decisions that you make about your health? How is your social circle impacting your dietary choices? How is your family tradition impacting your approach or thoughts about health and fitness? How is growing up as an athlete impacting that?

Sometimes it's hard to shake our competitive nature. We want to go hard, hard, hard. But as we get older and life changes and we become wives or mothers, or whatever our goals may be beyond that, it becomes challenging. It can get hard to adjust to not having that same structure that we're used to as athletes. The great side of being an athlete is that you are disciplined and you have the time prioritization, but then when that changes in the working world, it's like, "Where does that fit in?"

My goal and my vision with my clients is to really connect the dots between your outside environment, how that's impacting your internal environment, and the decisions you're making about how you approach and handle and manage your health and wellness. It sounds like a lot but, again, you can't compartmentalize your life. If you're dealing with stress over here, how is that impacting your fitness life?

All of that is together, and I want to help people see that in a very realistic way that they can understand. Then, it helps them to prioritize changing it or fixing it, if that's a necessary thing for them.

What are some skills that you would say are absolutely necessary to be competitive and to stay relative in your career?

Joi Madison: This is something I talk about. I mentor young girls, as well, through my company. It used to be, probably a lot of their parents, you graduate, you get a job, you work that job until you retire, and that's your life. That's not the case anymore. It's very much about bouncing around. A lot of it is creating your own lane, making your own job, working for yourself. There're lots of ways to create and be in control of your whole everything.

I think what's important is to always be clear about why. There's going to be a million different how's. You can get caught up in the how, and that can pull you away from your why. I didn't get into this to do marketing. Marketing is an important part of my job, but if I get caught up in the how, like the marketing, then my why gets lost. Then, I'm not relevant anymore because I've not stayed on top of what makes me, me in this industry.

The fitness industry, especially in L.A., is incredibly saturated. Everybody wants to look good. You've got to compete with the shakes and the waist trainers, and all these other things that are giving you a quick fix.

I would say to the young graduates who are getting ready to graduate and are entering the working world to become very clear about what impact you want to make. Then, be ready to do that in a range of different ways. It may not look like whatever you think it looks like right now. You've got to be open to that. Similar to a game-time situation, where you have your plays, you've got the X's and O's, and coach told you to do whatever you're going to do. When the game starts and things start happening, you have to be able to make decisions on the court, in the pool, on the field, on the floor, wherever you are, responding to the scenario as it's playing out in that moment. To make the best of whatever it's going to be for your intended goal, which is to win the game or the meet.

What are the final pieces of advice you would like to share with current female student-athletes?

Joi Madison: Be clear about your intentions and your why. I give three words: clarity, honesty, and willingness. Be clear about what it is you want. Be honest about what it's going to take to get there. Then, be willing to do what it takes.

Go into whatever you're going to do with those three things in mind, and just be willing to gun it out. Whatever that requires of you, with your self-care of course, that's the way of the world now. The world is moving so quickly, we don't have time to settle. We have to be ready to go.

Joi Madison's Contact Information:
Email: info@eatsleepsweat.com
Facebook: facebook.com/ESSfitness
Twitter: @eat_sleep_sweat
Instagram: @eat_sleep_sweat
YouTube: EAT.SLEEP.SWEAT.
Website: www.eatsleepsweat.com

Chapter 10: LISA MICELI-STANDAGE

Current occupation: Owner of Eco Fit Equipment and Fitness Design Consultant for Advanced Exercise.

Where did you go to college and what sport did you play?

Lisa Miceli-Standage: I played basketball at Truman State University.

What do you think would be some great advice for those young women going down that path?

Lisa Miceli-Standage: I think trying to explain to them that they don't have to go to a Division I school. They should just really pick a school that works best for them, and what's going to work best for them in their future. At 18, I don't think anybody really knows what the heck they're going to be doing when they're 35, but at the same time, it's great to be able to go to a school where you can connect on a lot of different levels.

If you're that athlete that's going to play Division I sports, that's awesome, and I cheer that on 110%, but that's not the end all be all. If there're opportunities for any of these athletes to be able to play a

Division II, Division III, taking that as an opportunity is definitely going to benefit their careers going forward.

How did you decide where to go to college?

Lisa Miceli-Standage: I decided to go to Truman because that's where I wanted to go to school, and I actually didn't go there to play basketball. I was a four-sport athlete in high school and played everything, and I didn't get recruited by the schools that I actually thought I would. For me, I just had a little bit of a maybe "I'll just go to school and go to school." That happened, and it didn't last very long because after I got there and I realized I was a student and playing every intramural sport that they offered, I realized it was probably best that I attempt to be a part of a team again. For me, it was a little bit of an unconventional way of doing things, but I went there because I connected with the school. I connected with the people, and I was still able to walk on the basketball team and it worked out insanely well.

What was your major and why did you select that particular major?

Lisa Miceli-Standage: I majored in Business Administration. I had both a Marketing and Management degree. I think why just comes down to the fact that I knew I'd always want to be in a form of business. I grew up with my mom having been in business as in real estate, and a VP of a real estate company, so I always saw that and I was always inspired to do the same. I wanted to work in a big fancy office, so I thought that's what you were supposed to do.

I actually thought I would be a sports agent, and go on to get my law degree. Soon after I started taking law class and the LSAT, I thought, "Maybe I'm going to have to find a different direction in life," but yeah. I mean, you're green, and you're young, and you don't really know until you start to get into it. I chose business, and it's always been something I've been most interested in.

What are some factors that impacted your career path? You said you've gone through a progression, so what has that been like for you?

Lisa Miceli-Standage: It's been very interesting, that's for sure. I graduated from college after having played sports, or I was on the team, and the career counselor came to our games and she was like, "What are you going to do? What are you going to do? What are you going to do?" I was like, "Well, I'm not going to go to law school anymore. That's not happening, so I don't know. I should get into sales probably." Who knew?

I think at the time I was considering getting into pharmaceutical sales, or medical sales, that was super hot, and everybody wanted to do that, right? I needed a job, so I went home from college. I had a college degree, and I took a job at a local gym working as a front desk person for $8.67, which I like to tell everybody because my parents thought, "What in the heck? You went to school. What are you doing?" It was really just supposed to be something to get me through the summer as I was prospecting for a career.

Within a year and a half, I was managing multiple clubs, and moved out to California, and was a district manager. I was like, "Well, shoot. This is a career. This is a great career." Then I fell in love with it. It definitely spoke to my personality. It spoke to what I wanted to do. I was very passionate about all of it. It all has kind of full circle continued on from there.

How do you go from being the front desk person to managing multiple districts, and regions, and people?

Lisa Miceli-Standage: I think you just work really hard. Some people think they're too good for this, or too good for that, or that's not good enough, or however you want to say it. I think I was just so humble in the fact that I just wanted to work, and I got up every day and I did what they asked me to do.

At 24 years old, when they asked me to be a district manager, I was like, "Yes!" All of it came down to the fact that I was just working my tail off. I think that's the really awesome thing about athletes. Most athletes I meet, they're not afraid to work. They get up every day and do what's asked of them, and if something doesn't go well, they get up the next day and try it again. Yeah, it just I think is a work ethic probably scenario.

Did you know that you wanted to be a leader in the organization?

Lisa Miceli-Standage: Within about six months of working there, I did. Yeah, within a very short period of time, I knew that that's what I wanted to do and I think having the open communication with the people above me at the time, telling them that this is where I saw myself and this is what I wanted to do also helped—and helping myself be in that position when that opportunity came available.

Did you feel like you were ready for the position when you went to California?

Lisa Miceli-Standage: Heck yeah! I was just green and so ready. It was very nerve-wracking. I moved out to California. I actually forced one of my friends to move so that I didn't have to live alone. I didn't have a place; otherwise, I was living in my car for a day, which was super exciting. For a couple of days I guess I should say. Yeah, no. I didn't really think of it like that.

I was just so excited and motivated to do a really good job that I didn't think about it until I was in that moment and I was amongst all these people. Everybody that worked for me was much older than me, and there was quite a bit of a reality check that had to happen. I had to adjust my train of thought and how I reacted to things pretty quickly because if I started to act like the 24-year-old, I wasn't going to get a heck of a lot of respect in my position.

What are some other challenges that you faced in that role or other roles that you've had?

Lisa Miceli-Standage: I think the biggest challenge that I faced in that role and then any others I've played is just working amongst a lot of men. Not that that's a bad thing, but I've always been in a very male-dominated type of job and industry, and I think the challenge is to be able to handle yourself in a professional manner to be respected, but know that you're going to be challenged in a much different way than maybe some of your counterparts are, and embrace it.

I think that when you know that you can do that, then all things continue to go well, but there are some moments that have happened and challenges that I've had because of that that now I look back and think, "Maybe I could've handled that differently, or maybe I should've done that differently," but you don't really know until you live through it.

After going through these challenges, what changes did you make?

Lisa Miceli-Standage: I went back to home with the gym that I worked for, and things just weren't working out all that well based on some of those things that I just had mentioned. I saw myself not growing as much as I originally had with the organization, and that's deeply rooted in who I am. I want to see an upward trajectory.

I think all athletes probably feel the same way, or most of them might, in that, once you become stagnant or complacent, it gets a little tough to stay. I get jittery. I'm like, "Okay what's the next step, or where's the next move? What's the next opportunity? Where are we going from here?" There was just a lot of changes within the organization that I didn't see were too positive.

That's when we parted ways, and I started my own business at that point, Advanced Exercise Equipment. I always just told myself, "I'm really good at getting up and working really hard," so working for myself wasn't really that much of a challenge. It is a challenge, because then, all of a sudden, it's all on you. You take on a little bit more, but overall it's worth it.

The things that I learned within that helped me get into that position where I am now with my company, and growing into another company, and seeing opportunities in different ways, and a lot of it just has to do with that experience that I did have.

Did you know that you always wanted to stay around athletics, or did it just happen because of your first job out of college?

Lisa Miceli-Standage: It was always something I wanted to do. I think having been just totally inundated with sports my whole life, it made sense for me. I have one older brother that I'm pretty sure he thought I was a little boy until we were about 15, no joke. I enjoyed sports. I grew up in a neighborhood with all boys. That's just what I knew, and I think there's a comfort level that comes along with that. Then there's also that passion that goes alongside it.

I look around me now and I think, "Could I have done this, or could I have done that, or could I have been this?" Yeah, I could, but I truly enjoy what I get to do every day. The people I get to work with, and what I get to talk about, and I know that part of my growth and my career also stemmed from taking a chance on my goals.

I took a little hiatus from having my own business when I started working for Spalding. I thought, "That's what I really want to do." I get to work for a sporting goods company? That's super cool, right? Growing up, we have Rawlings here in St. Louis, and I always thought if I didn't make it as the sports agent, I would work for Rawlings, because that's hometown sports, right? When I got an opportunity to work for Spalding, I did take it, and so I kind of let the other stuff go by the wayside to a point but knew that I think my passion was always there, and that I would be going back to it.

Within my opportunity with Spalding and working in that organization and with those people, I learned so much more there that I would've never learned had I not taken that opportunity. Then, like what you said earlier, people take these risks, or they take on these positions they know nothing about. I took a job that I was totally clueless about, and it ended up serving me very well. It served my career very well. It served a lot of things. It's been wonderful.

How did you decide which strategic moves to make for your career path?

Lisa Miceli-Standage: Yeah, I think it's all strategy. It's hard to say because the strategy behind it was I wanted to excel in this business. Whether it be in the sports and fitness industry, or just the sporting goods industry, I wanted to excel. I wanted to make an impact. I thought that working for an organization like Spalding in that sporting goods environment would really teach me a lot about how the manufacturing process works.

At this point in my life, I do truly believe that that will benefit me as I continue to grow in my career. I do think that it was strategic. I think that if somebody would've asked me to come on and do a job in IT consulting, I would've probably said no. That's just not up my alley, but being able to work within this industry, and to continue to build on that, yeah that was all strategic.

What are some mistakes you've made along the way and how have you bounced back from them?

Lisa Miceli-Standage: I make mistakes every day, I'm sure. I think that you have to take risks, and sometimes those risks don't always create a reward, but hopefully, you learned something from it. From pinpointing one particular mistake, there's probably 18 million so it's hard to determine. I have to tell you, I've been thinking about it for a while, and I was like, "I don't know." I just can't think of one particular mistake, because I know I do them all the time.

I think the mistakes that I do make haven't been detrimental to my career, or my life, or anything like that. It's more so just, maybe if I would think through the process more, or think through the outcome more thoroughly, then I would have had a different outcome. A lot of times, as an entrepreneur in what I do, you move so fast, so that's when mistakes get made. I tell Jen, my business partner, all the time I say, "We just need to slow down. Take a step back. Analyze this client. Figure out what's the best solution for them," instead of just going quick all the time.

It sounds like you live a pretty busy life. How do you de-stress?

Lisa Miceli-Standage: Oh, you know I do live a busy life, but I will tell you this one thing. I really love the balance in my life. I have a new baby, and that has slowed me down a lot. She's six months old now, but it's definitely put life in perspective. I think it's great. I appreciate spending time with my friends and my family. We barbecue, just like the basic things. I can go for a long workout, or a good hike, or any of that kind of stuff—it's very important—but at the same time, I know that my family life and in my life, we do have a lot of balance, which is very beneficial.

What are some ways that you use what you've learned in sport in your day-to-day life?

Lisa Miceli-Standage: At the end of the day, as an athlete, you practice, practice, practice for a big game, or you're constantly trying to improve your skills. I think that daily, that's just what it is. I feel like in the business that I'm constantly trying to make myself better, and trying to be a better company to my clients, and a better partner to various organizations. You don't get too beat down because, in the sales industry, you get told no a lot, so you just get back up and you just go.

People are going to tell you no all the time, or you're not going to win every deal, and you're not going to be the perfect fit for every single person that you're trying to work with. You get up and you just go, and I think if you just continue to do the work, the outcome is going to happen. The positive outcome is going to happen.

There're so many things about being an athlete that I think benefit just the day-to-day in the world. Like being able to take on a bunch of different things at once. As an entrepreneur, I have to give my business partner, Jen, some credit, because she handles our books, because it would be a disaster if that was on me. From doing marketing, and various networking, and you have to be so many different hats for so many different people. We work in a lot of different industries that also adjust how you are to a client. Working with a coach is a lot different than working with a developer, and when you're in that situation, you just have to know how to play all different parts, different roles.

How do you handle conflict? Conflict's inevitable when you're dealing with a client or your teammates who you work with. How do you handle that? What's some advice?

Lisa Miceli-Standage: You know, I always think that—handling conflict, mostly with work. I don't really have a conflict, I guess otherwise; but even having some emotional intelligence, I think, is really important. I think that's probably a very broad statement, but something I've learned over the years is that it is important to understand yourself emotionally and how you react to things. In line with what I said before, think about things before you react to determine what that outcome looks like. I think becoming less defensive in a lot of different scenarios is very helpful in resolving conflict.

I'm a pretty straight shooter kind of person, and I just tell people like, "Here's the deal, and this is who I am, or this is what we got going on," so you shoot me straight, I'll shoot you straight back. Generally speaking, if I'm not getting that kind of back and forth with somebody, I just try to ease into that to gain their trust, but the conflict part's kind of difficult. Being a small company now, there's not a whole lot of conflict. Just try to be emotionally intelligent about how you react to things I think is most important.

What would your advice be to your 21 or 22-year-old self when you were graduating?

Lisa Miceli-Standage: I would probably tell her to enjoy the process, and not take everything so seriously. I would tell myself that everything's going to be fine, just continue to work hard, and be true to myself and be true to who I am, and know that with the hard work and everything else, it's not going to always be easy. There's going to be some things that happen that are just little bumps in the road, but they're not the end all be all, and to continue to do what I do. Just do what you do, and everything will be fine.

What are the final pieces of advice you would like to share with current female student-athletes?

Lisa Miceli-Standage: Just being humble. A really big thing that I see with young people that get out of school is that they play a sport and that's awesome, but that doesn't make you invincible. There's a lot of people out there that have accomplished a lot of things. I think just being humble and confident at the same time is so important, and understanding that there's so much to learn. There's so much to learn even after school. That's just the beginning, really.

Lisa Miceli-Standage's Contact Information:
Email: lmiceli@advancedexercise.com
Facebook: Lisa Miceli-Standage
Facebook: Advanced Exercise Equipment MO & So. IL
Facebook: Eco Fit Equipment

Chapter 11: FERNANDA DE PAOLA

Current occupation: Founder of Athlete Booster.

What college did you attend and what sport did you play?

Fernanda de Paola (Spanish): Jugué baloncesto. Instituto Tenológico y de Estudios Superiores de Monterrey Campus Monterrey donde estudié mi carrera. Está ubicado en el estado de Monterrey, Nuevo León, en el norte del país. Universidad de las Américas Puebla, donde estudié mi maestría. Está ubicada en el estado de Puebla, Puebla, en el sur del país.

Fernanda de Paola (English): I played basketball at Institute of Technology and Higher Studies, Monterrey Campus, Monterrey, where I studied my career, in the state of Monterrey, Nuevo Leon in northern Mexico. Universidad de las Américas Puebla, where I studied my masters; it is located in the state of Puebla, in the south of the country.

What was your greatest accomplishment in your athletic career?

Fernanda de Paola (Spanish): Sin duda el logro más grande fue haber tenido la oportunidad de compartir campeonatos con varias generaciones de jugadoras, entre las que se encontraban varias

Seleccionadas Nacionales que representaron a México en Justas internacionales como Panamericanos, Universiada Mundial. Y el logro más poderoso, pudiera ponerle ese adjetivo, fue el lograr una carrera y maestría gracias al deporte.

Fernanda de Paola (English): Undoubtedly, the greatest achievement was to have had the opportunity to share championships with several generations of players, including several National Selected teams who represented Mexico in international competitions like Pan American World. And the most powerful achievement was to get a career and expertise through sport.

What was your major and why did you select that major?

Fernanda de Paola (Spanish): Soy Licenciada en Mercadotecnia y Maestra en Administración de Empresas con Especialidad en Dirección Estratégica. Fue una historia curiosa el cómo elegí a carrera de Mercadotecnia, se las platico:

Cuando estaba en preparatoria siempre fui una buena alumna, no la mejor, pero me consideraba aplicada y mis maestros en ocasiones me lo decían. Al acercarse la fecha de graduación de preparatoria la clásica pregunta es: ¿Dónde y qué vas a estudiar? Yo había pensado en Mercadotecnia porque veía el área de oportunidad de que, durante la carrera y al finalizar la misma iba a tener varias opciones de hacia dónde enfocar la material de Mercadotecnia (ya que es muy amplia), entonces yo contestaba muy segura que eso iba a estudiar y mis maestros me decían que cómo, que podia estudiar algo mejor, algo más difícil, prácticamente que iba a ser un "talento" desperdiciado... Y la verdad es que me dejé influenciar. Presenté el exámen de admisión de la Universidad y en la hoja de solicitud puse que aplicaba para Administración Financiera... Pasé el examen y continué con mi proceso. Pero pensaba mucho, bastante diría yo, en que si realmente eso era lo que quería, porque a decir verdad no soy taaaan buena con los números, creo que eso fue lo que más pesó y 2 semanas antes de entrar a clases me cambié de Carrera a Mercadotecnia... Bien recuerdo que la entonces Directora de Carrera, Adriana Carranza, me dijo: Bienvenida, haz visto la luz. Y sí, no me arrepiento ni un segundo.

Fernanda de Paola (English): I have a degree in Marketing and Master in Business Administration with a concentration in Strategic Management. It was a curious story how I chose Marketing career.

When I was in high school, I was always a good student, not the best, but I applied what my teachers told me sometimes. As the date of school graduation approached, a classic question was asked: "Where and what are you going to study?"

I had thought of marketing (material marketing) because I saw it as an area that would have several options of where to focus in the end (as it is wide), and so I answered. Back then in school, I'm very sure my teacher was like, "How? You could study something better, something more difficult; practically, it would be a 'talent' wasted ..." and the truth is that I let myself be influenced.

I registered for the entrance exam at the University and in the application form, I applied for financial management. I passed the exam and continued my process. But I thought a lot, enough I would say, if that really was what I wanted because I was not so good with numbers. I think that was what weighed me down. Two weeks before entering classes, I changed to Carrera Marketing. Well, I remember that the then Director of Carrera, Adriana Carranza, told me: "Welcome, seen the light beam?" And yes, I do not regret a second.

What factors impacted your decision to select your current career path?

Fernanda de Paola (Spanish):: Como comentaba en la pregunta anterior, en un inicio me dejé llevar por lo que la gente a mi alrededor esperaba de mi. Pero sinceramente pensé: Yo soy la que voy a estudiar esa carrera, ellos no van a desvelarse conmigo, no van a estar insatisfechos si yo me siento insatisfecha estudiando eso, el éxito no está definido con base en dónde te van a pagar más, sino en dónde o en qué estarás poniendo tu tiempo, tu esfuerzo y, principalmente, dónde estarás viviendo de tu pasión, tu profesión. Y al final del día la decision que más pesó para elegir lo "correcto" fue la decision propia. Gracias a Dios tengo una familia que me apoya en todo y nunca juzgó el camino que iba a tomar.

Fernanda de Paola (English): As I mentioned in the previous question, initially I got carried away by what people around me expected of me. But honestly, I thought, I'm the one going to study, they will not unravel me, they will not be dissatisfied if I feel unsatisfied studying.

Success is not defined based on where you are going to pay more, but where or what you are putting your time, your effort and, mainly, where you'll be living your passion, your profession. And at the end of the day, the decision heaviest weighed on me to choose the "right" proper decision. Thank God I have a family that supports me in everything and never judged the path it would take.

How did you go about securing your first job after your finished playing and what was that process?

Fernanda de Paola (Spanish): Ahora que me voy en retrospectiva, pienso en que siempre he sido una persona que le gusta mucho expresarse, cuando está bien, cuando está mal, lo que piensa, opina. Y durante la carrera siempre fui así, el auge de las redes sociales se volvió una plataforma increíble para mi jaja porque así podia expresarme y llegar a mucha gente. Desde hace varios años tengo mi blog, mismo que igual durante mi carrera lo mantuve activo por temporadas y fungió, y lo sigue haciendo, como una plataforma donde me puedo exponer, quién soy, de dónde vengo, qué hago, qué me gusta, qué opino. Aunado a eso me encanta conocer gente y saber qué hacen para ver cuál sera el siguiente proyecto.

Un día me contactó una persona que se llama Héctor Bache, Co-Fundador de la empresa de Consultoría Deportiva CMAS Athletes, precisamente por Facebook mediante un mensaje directo. Recuerdo que me platicó sobre la empresa (que en aquél entonces era meramente un proyecto y ahora ya es una compañía consolidada) y me hizo la invitación a conocer lo que se tenía para explorar de qué manera poder colaborar. Acepté y fui a Dallas, Texas a conocerlo a él y a Guillermo Zamarripa, Fundador de la empresa. Conocí el propósito de la empresa (el cual es apoyar a estudiantes-deportistas de todo el mundo para conseguir una beca deportiva-académica para estudiar preparatoria o Universidad en Estados Unidos) y la verdad es que rápidamente me sentí identificada, definitivamente es algo que hubiese querido que existiera en el tiempo en que yo iba a ingresar a Universidad para explorar el tener esa oportunidad de desenvolverme deportiva como académicamente en Estados Unidos.

Me dieron mucha confianza y también la oportunidad de poder empezar a trabajar de manera remota, ya que yo me iría a Puebla a realizar mis estudios de maestría. Y así fue como llegó mi primer trabajo.

En mi persona, las 2 claves importantes para lograr tener una transición exitosa fueron:

1. Trabajar en mi misma – Permitirme darme esa exposición hacia el mundo que está ahí afuera.

2. Tener un amplio círculo de personas que comparten mis mismos intereses – Eso es increíble, ya que cada vez vas encontrando un proyecto nuevo o vas integrando gente a tu proyecto personal.

Fernanda de Paola (English): Now that I'm back, I think I've always been a person who likes to express themselves, when it is bad, what he thinks he says. And during the race, I was always so. The rise of social networks presented an incredible platform for me because I could express myself and reach many people.

For several years, I have had my blog. Similarly, during my career, I kept active by serving as a platform where I can expose who I am, where I come from, what I do, what I like, what I think. In addition to that, I love to meet people and know what they do to see what the next project would be.

One day I was contacted by a person called Hector Bache, Co-Founder of the consulting firm CMAS Sports Athletes, through a direct message on Facebook. I remember I talked about the company (which at that time was merely a project and now is a consolidated company) and he offered me an invitation to know what needed to be explored and how to collaborate. I accepted and went to Dallas, Texas to meet him and Guillermo Zamarripa, founder of the company.

I knew the purpose of the company (which is to support student-athletes from around the world to get academic sports scholarship to study in high school or university in the United States) and the truth is that I quickly felt identified. It is definitely something that I had longed for at the time. I was going to enter University to explore the opportunity to deal with sports and academics in the United States. I got a lot of confidence and the opportunity to start working remotely because I would go to Puebla to do my MBA. And that was how it was—my first job.

For me, the two important keys to a successful transition were:

I worked on myself – I wanted to give myself that exposure to the world out there.

Having a wide circle of people who share same interests with me – That's amazing because it involves finding new projects or integrating people into your personal project.

What has been your career progression to the point you are at today?

Fernanda de Paola (Spanish): En CMAS Athletes permanecí por 2 años. Al terminar mi maestría en la Universidad de las Américas en el estado de Puebla me regresé a vivir a Monterrey, Nuevo León, donde había estudiado mi carrera. Al llegar aquí sí pensaba mucho en que quería seguir desempeñándome dentro de la industria deportiva y tuve la oportunidad de explorar varias opciones, donde una de ellas era precisamente dentro de la misma, en el retail deportivo. Gracias al apoyo y empuje del que ahora es mi jefe, Gerardo Alvarado y del Director de Mercadotecnia, Sergio Porras, logré formar parte del equipo de Mercadotecnia de Innovasport, retailer deportivo número 1 en México. Actualmente me desempeño en el área de marketing sensorial e innovación en retail, donde el propósito es mejorar la experiencia del consumidor en el punto de venta, además de colaborar y liderar proyectos que aportan valor a la compañía.

Al mismo tiempo, estoy empujando muy fuerte mi proyecto personal Athlete Booster, donde me enfoco en asesorar a atletas para que tengan una transición de la cancha a la vida "real" más efectiva y exitosa, este es como mi bebé y me pone contenta que más gente está abierta y dispuesta a colaborar.

Fernanda de Paola (English): As an athlete in CMAS, I stayed for two years. When I finished my master's at the University of the Americas in Puebla State, I moved back to Monterrey, Nuevo Leon, where I had studied my career. Upon arriving here, I didn't want to continue to function within the sports industry as I had the opportunity to explore several options; one of them was precisely the sports retail. Thanks to the support and push from my boss, Gerardo Alvarado, and Marketing Director, Sergio Porras.

I managed to join the team, Innovasport Marketing, No. 1 sports retailer in Mexico. I currently serve in the area of sensory marketing and innovation in retail, where the purpose is to improve the customer experience at the point of sale, as well as collaborating and leading projects that add value to the company.

At the same time, I'm pushing very hard my personal project—Athlete Booster—which focuses on advising athletes to have a transition from the court to the most effective and successful "real" life. This is like my baby and it makes me happy that more people are open and willing to collaborate.

What are your career goals?

Fernanda de Paola (Spanish): Siempre he pensado que uno debe tener un propósito de vida bien establecido, si es así todo lo que haces y en lo que te involucras girará en torno a éste y las satisfacciones no pararán. Mi propósito de vida es medir mi éxito con base al número de vidas que toco y esto busco constantemente trasladarlo a mi lado profesional.

En Innovasport mi objetivo es crecer dentro de mi área, aportando valor a largo plazo para la compañía. Mis días los enfoco en ello buscando no solamente tener un impacto positivo dentro del equipo de Mercadotecnia, sino también en cualquiera de mis compañeros de las demás áreas que me permita impulsarle de manera profesional.

En cuanto a mi proyecto Athletes Booster, mi sueño es poder ser aquella persona en la que los atletas piensen cuando quieran recibir algún consejo para trasladar sus habilidades más allá del juego, al área profesional y poder apoyarles de manera tangible a que tengan éxito en sus profesiones. Tengo muchas ideas en cuanto a este tema y seguiré persiguiendo el hacerlas realidad.

Fernanda de Paola (English): I've always thought that one should have a well-established life purpose; if so, everything you do and what you engage revolves around it and satisfaction becomes endless. My life purpose is to measure my success based on the number of lives I touch and move—this is what I constantly seek in my professional side.

In Innovasport, my goal is to grow within my area, providing long-term value for the company. The focus is on looking not only to have a positive impact on the marketing team but also with any of my colleagues from other areas to allow me to drive them professionally.

As for my project, Athletes Booster, my dream is to be that person that athletes think of when they want to receive any advice to transfer their skills beyond the game, the professional area and to support them in a tangible way to succeed in their professions. I have many ideas regarding this issue and will continue pursuing them into reality.

What are some challenges you've faced as you've made different career choices?

Fernanda de Paola (Spanish): Ha sido grande el reto. No es fácil de repente dejar un trabajo con la incertidumbre de si el siguiente irá a llenarte o si encontrarás aquél trabajo que has estado deseando. En mi historia personal puedo decir que he sido afortunada, ya que he formado parte de proyectos u organizaciones que me han llenado y que donde estoy hoy me siento contenta, agradecida y feliz por hacer de mi pasión mi profesión.

Un consejo que quisiera comentar, como comenté en una pregunta anterior, es que trabajemos en nosotros mismos, en construir nuestra persona, nuestro lado profesional, que conectemos con gente que comparte nuestras mismas pasiones y que sean catapultas, no anclas que nos frenen y al mismo tiempo nosotros impulsar a alguien más en el camino.

Fernanda de Paola (English): The challenge has been great. It is not easy to suddenly leave a job with the uncertainty of whether the next will go to fill or find that job you've been wanting. In my personal history, I can say I've been lucky because I've been part of projects or organizations that have filled me to where I am today.

I feel happy, grateful and excited to make my passion my profession. One tip I would like to comment, as I mentioned in an earlier question, is that we work on ourselves, build our person , our professional side , we connect with people who share our same passions and are catapults, not anchors that hold us back while we push someone else down the road.

Name a time you made a mistake and how you came back from it?

Fernanda de Paola (Spanish): He cometido muchos errores, sin duda. Sin embargo no tengo uno que ahora tenga muy presente o muy claro. Pero me gustaría compartir un mensaje que tiene que ver con los errores y que hace poco compartí en mi blog en Medium...

Para no hacerles muy larga la historia, en Innovasport constantemente estoy involucrada en proyectos de los cuales forman parte Directores de áreas y Dirección General. En uno de ellos, sucedió un pequeño detalle donde compartí algunos archivos erroneos que retrasaron el avance del mismo, yo no me había percatado hasta que una Directora comentó en el correo ese detalle y yo vi el caso y envié los archivos correctos, disculpándome por la información errónea. Cuando mando ese correo, un compañero también involucrado en el mismo, se acerca conmigo y me dice que por qué puse "me equivoqué" si estaban copiados todos los Directores y Dirección General, y yo le contesté que no se me hacía algo de lo que me tuviera que preocupar o avergonzar.

La moraleja con la que me quedo es: ¿por qué nos da miedo aceptar que nos equivocamos?, ¿por qué tenemos que "ocultar" un error?, ¿por qué le tenemos que otorgar a otro ser humano ese poder de juzgarnos por una equivocación?, ¿por qué tenemos miedo a "mostrarnos débiles" si los errores son las armas más poderosas que nos enseñan a ser mejores? No tengamos miedo de decir "me equivoqué", que nada pasa, y uno aprende.

Fernanda de Paola (English): I have made many mistakes, no doubt. However, I have one that now is very present and very clear. But I would like to share a message that has to do with the mistakes and recently, I shared it on my blog as a medium...

To make very long history in Innovasport, I am constantly involved in projects with Directors and General Management. In one of them, I shared some erroneous files that slowed progress. I had not noticed until a Director commented on that detail via email and I saw the case and sent the correct files, apologizing for the misinformation. When I sent that email, a partner also involved in it approached me and asked me why I put "I was wrong" if all of the Directors and General Management were copied. I said that was something I didn't have to worry about or feel ashamed of.

The moral here is we have to think about why we are afraid to accept that we were wrong. Why do we have to "hide" a mistake? Why do we have to give another human being that power to judge by a mistake? Why are we afraid to "show weakness" if errors are the most powerful weapons that teach us to be better? Do not be afraid to say, "I was wrong"; nothing happens, and you learn.

In what ways do you de-stress from your work environment?

Fernanda de Paola (Spanish): Cuando llego a estar estresada por lo regular me muevo a trabajar a otro espacio distinto a donde acostumbro estar, para cambiar un poco el ambiente. Escucho música y me relajo. Como muy bien, suena raro pero es un factor que influye en cómo avanzamos y tomamos el día.

Fernanda de Paola (English): When I become stressed, usually, I move to work in a different space from where I usually stay—to change the environment a bit. I listen to music and relax. As well, it sounds weird but it is a factor that influences how we move forward and take the day.

When you do not agree with the morals, ethics, or policies in your work environment, how do you handle it? Or, what methods do you use to resolve conflict?

Fernanda de Paola (Spanish): Precisamente sí me llegó a suceder una cuestión de ese tipo en cierto punto que estoy consciente de que en su momento no la manejé tal vez de la manera "correcta", mas creo que es cuestión de madurez, de adaptación y de conocer distintos ambientes laborales.

El desarrollar el sentido de empatía y de saber hasta dónde es viable que uno se involucre o cuestione o enfrente son aspectos importantes que hay que trabajar constantemente.

Fernanda de Paola (English): Precisely, yes I had that happen and at the time, it was not handled perhaps the "right" way, but I think it's a matter of maturity, adaptation and learn ing different work environments. The development of a sense of empathy and how far it is feasible that one is involved, questions, and faces the issue are important aspects that a person has to work on constantly.

What are some examples of the ways you've used what you've learned in sports in your day-to-day life?

Fernanda de Paola (Spanish):

1. Trabajo en equipo: básico, fundamental. Probablemente yo soy buena para los tiros de 3 puntos pero no para los bloqueos, pero sé que al lado mío tengo un compañero que es bueno para los

bloqueos. Colaborar, apoyar, crecer junto a un equipo es uno de los regalos que el deporte te da y que trasladas automáticamente a la vida diaria.

2. Escuchar: saber que habrá alguien, un coach, un mentor que me dirá si voy bien, qué me falla, cómo puedo corregirlo, y escucharle con atención es un factor clave para poder crecer tanto como deportista como profesionista.

3. Vivir la vida como si fuera el ultimo cuarto del partido: en México jugamos los partidos de basquetbol en 4 cuartos de 10 minutos cada uno. Formé parte de juegos donde, por razones relacionadas con la comodidad, el exceso de confianza o el tema de "queda mucho tiempo por jugar aún", nos metíamos en problemas porque jugábamos muy relajadas durante 2 o 3 cuartos del juego y en el último entrábamos en apuro. Eso me enseñó a vivir la vida como si fuera el ultimo cuarto, desde el primero, pero no apurada, sino aplicada, enfocada precisamente para no llegar al final a querer forzar las cosas con la probabilidad de no obtener la victoria.

Fernanda de Paola (English):

1. Teamwork: basic, fundamental. I'm probably good for 3-point shots but not for blocks, but I know next to me I have a partner that is good for blocks. Collaborate, support, grow with a team is one of the gifts that sport gives you and this automatically translates to everyday life.

2. Listen: knowing that there is someone, a coach, a mentor who will tell me if I'm right, what's wrong with me, how I can correct it, and to listen carefully is a key to growing both as an athlete as a professional.

3. Live life as if it were the last quarter of the game: in Mexico, basketball games are played in four quarters of 10 minutes each. I was part of games where, for reasons related to comfort, overconfidence or theme of "much time to play yet," we got into trouble because we played very relaxed for 2 or 3 quarters of the game and the last entered in trouble. That taught me to live life as if it were the last quarter from the first, not rushed but applied precisely with the focus on reaching the end without wanting to force things with the probability of victory.

What skill sets are most transferable for attaining a job in the current market?

Fernanda de Paola (Spanish): Liderazgo: el poder empujar un proyecto y más cuando involucra a mucha gente es una cualidad que sin duda estamos buscando allá afuera, en las nuevas generaciones de atletas. Personas que tienen esta cualidad te dan confianza y crecen rápido.

Inteligencia emocional: el hecho de saber reaccionar de manera positiva ante ciertas circunstancias difíciles, cuando un proyecto no avanza, cuando no se toma la mejor decision. Es un tema relativamente nuevo pero que sin duda viene muy fuerte, el tener tolerancia ante la frustación o momentos no agradables es un factor importante y, como comenté anteriormente, mucho tiene que ver con la madurez que uno va adquiriendo en el camino.

Fernanda de Paola (English): Leadership: to push a project, and when it involves a lot of people, is a quality that people are certainly looking out there in the new generations of athletes. People who have this quality give you confidence and grow fast.

Emotional intelligence: the knowledge of to react positively to certain difficult circumstances when a project does not advance, when not making the best decision. It is a relatively new issue but it certainly is very strong; having tolerance for frustration or pleasant moments is an important factor and as mentioned above, much has to do with the maturity that one acquires on the way.

What are the final pieces of advice you would like to share with current female student-athletes?

Fernanda de Paola (Spanish): Me gustaría volver a repetir mi consejo: trabaja en ti, tienes un gran potencial más allá de las canchas, de los campos de juego, tienes el potencial de convertirte poco a poco en tu mejor version y de posteriormente ayudar a más gente a que se convierta en la suya. Aprovecha todas las enseñanzas del deporte y encuentra la manera de apoyarlo desde donde te encuentres, crea, cree, involucra, prueba, apuéstale a tus sueños y a tus pasiones y seguramente vivirás una vida plena y dejarás un legado y una semilla sembrada en más de una persona de las nuevas generaciones.

Fernanda de Paola (English): I would like to repeat my advice: "Work on you; you have great potential beyond the tennis, golf game. You have the potential to gradually become your best version and then help more people.

Take advantage of all the teachings of sport and find a way to support it from wherever you are. Belief involves tests. Follow your dreams, your passions and live a full life. Leave a legacy and a seed planted in more than one person of the new generations."

Fernanda de Paola's Contact Information:
Email: hello@athletebooster.com
Facebook: Fernanda Corral
Twitter: @fernandadepalo
Instagram: Fernanda de Palo
Website: athletebooster.com

Chapter 12: ERICA SMITH

Current Occupation: Founder of Second Wind Enterprises and Co-Owner of Machine Elite Basketball Academy.

Where did you attend college, what sport you played?

Erica Smith: I went to Southern Illinois University, Carbondale. I played basketball for four years.

What's your greatest accomplishment in your athletic career?

Erica Smith: As a team, the greatest accomplishment, definitely, would be winning a conference championship my sophomore year. That was our first one in 18 years at SIUC and first one in Missouri Valley. That definitely was one of my greatest accomplishments as a student-athlete.

Individually, I think it was definitely being one of three guards to lead their team in rebounding for three consecutive years. One, because I played point guard in college, so I was the furthest away from the basket. More so, I think—when trying to teach kids nowadays—that rebounding isn't a thing of skill. It's a thing of the heart. It's a thing of will. That just shows the persistence that you're going to go after what you want. The basketball is what I wanted.

Talk a little bit about the academic side of college. What did you major in, and why did you select that major?

Erica Smith: In college, I actually double-majored in management and marketing. My emphasis was in entrepreneurship—the management and marketing side—because I love the relationship side of business. I think there is a great reward in building relationships in the business world. Not only for each company but for your personal growth. Then, the focus on entrepreneurship because I knew that I always wanted to own my company, so I got as much knowledge as I possibly could while I was in college to do so.

When did you realize that you wanted to own your own company? Did you have an "a-ha" moment?

Erica Smith: That's funny. I actually had a candy store when I was five. As a kid, I told my mom I wanted a candy store. She went to Sam's Club and then got all the candy and all that kind of stuff. She made me run it, so at five or six it's not like she's running this candy store. I could be outside playing and somebody comes to the door and they want to buy some candy and she's calling me in like, "Hey, you got a customer. Come take care of this." I think that early on, she never gave me anything. She instilled into me that if you want it, you're going to have to work for it. That just built a passion for me always wanting to have my own.

How did you go about securing your first job after college? You actually went to work when you finished college, you didn't start your own business immediately, correct?

Erica Smith: Yes and no. In college, my best friend and I had a textbook rental business, MyBookBuyer.com; we launched that when I was my senior year in college. We did a few college tours through the Missouri area, the Illinois area, just going and promoting that. When I got finished playing basketball, I actually had planned to go play overseas. Then my mom got sick the summer following my senior year, so I made a choice to stay and then pursued my master's degree.

I went on and got a master's in Sociology. Following that, my heart was still in the business side of things. As much as I love society and what's going on and the relationships and how we respond to things, my heart was still in business. I decided to take a position as a management trainee with Sherwin-Williams, and I secured that position actually through the Athletes Network. A phenomenal site that connects student athletes with other student athletes that are in companies.

The website lists a lot of different job opportunities, so I saw the different ones for Sherwin-Williams. I actually applied for a position in Milwaukee and one in Orlando, as a management trainee. The next day, the recruiter from Milwaukee called me and did an interview with me. At that time, I told her I had applied in Orlando as well, and she was like, "If you decide that you want to do that, I know the recruiter down there. I'll put in a good word for you." I thought about it for a day and I called her back and I was like, "Milwaukee or Orlando? Hmmm. I want to go to Orlando." I ended up doing a Skype interview with the district manager in Orlando which turned out to be a great fit. He's one of the best mentors I've had in the business world. It was a good fit for me.

What was your role with Sherwin-Williams and why did you decide to work for this company?

Erica Smith: Sherwin-Williams is a phenomenal company. I enjoyed my time there, but my reason for doing the management trainee program with Sherwin-Williams is because it's one of the most respected in the country. As a college student, I did an internship with Enterprise, which again is another very respected management trainee program. If I was going to do it, I wanted to be with some of the best companies and get the most knowledge possible.

That was my plan with Sherwin-Williams because you start out, as a management trainee, and you have that title but you don't really have any kind of responsibility. You're learning the ropes. Then you progress to an Assistant Manager of the store. Then depending on your ability and your desire and drive to push forward to be a manager, you have that opportunity as well. I was in Orlando and I was an Assistant Manager at two different stores in Orlando, and then accepted a position back here in St. Louis as a store manager. I managed the store here for about a year before I moved on.

What did you learn from your management experience?

Erica Smith: So many things. One of the biggest things, though, I think is how to deal with different personalities and how to bring the best out of people. In Orlando, the store that I actually trained in, I had a phenomenal leader who would give you anything, any kind of knowledge, but he threw you to the fire, which I love. He didn't hold me back. He let me go run. If I had any questions I would come to him, but he let me do my thing.

Then when I became an assistant at a different store, one of my biggest challenges was I'm a go-getter, I want to succeed, I want to do all those things, and the person that was in management there was comfortable in the position that they were in. My district manager and I talked a lot about "How do you manage up?" You're in this position where you can't really step on any toes, but you also have to make sure that the surroundings that you're in are successful. I learned how to change the atmosphere where I was working to implement different things.

That was huge. Then when I was a manager, you have so many different personalities and so many things that drive different people. It was important to me, and I did this with every person that I brought onto my team, to figure out what was important to them, what motivated them, how they wanted to be managed, because some people need to be micromanaged and some people, you just need to let them go and do their thing. I always had those conversations with them in the beginning, and then we would follow up with those conversations. I think that definitely helped me going forward.

What factors should young athletes consider when deciding which organizations to work with?

Erica Smith: I get the question a lot. It's funny that you say that, because I get a question all the time, like, "Sherwin-Williams, why paint?" At the end of the day, I don't think that people realize that it's not about the product, so much as it's about the process and it's about what you can gain from that experience. I think that even when I left there I went to work for a company called Randstad where I sold staffing solutions to different companies in the manufacturing industry.

Again, people were like, "Why the manufacturing industry?" It's not about that. I interviewed and placed people from our plant managers to inventory specialist to maintenance mechanics, operations managers. The wealth of knowledge that you gain from that is invaluable. It's not about the product. It's not about the industry. It's about what you can actually gain from that experience.

A lot of times athletes want to stay around athletics in their professional career. What made you decide that that wasn't the highest priority?

Erica Smith: I don't think that I separated the identity of an athlete. I think what I did is transfer those skill sets, transfer those things that I learned as an athlete into wherever I went. I probably wasn't dribbling a basketball in those settings, but I had to learn how to lead a team. I had to learn how to be aggressive in the right situations. I had to learn how to find the passion in something and run with that. I had to learn how to overcome obstacles. Everything that you do as an athlete, right? I had to transition those things.

I still was around sports because Machine Elite is basketball. I still fed that passion as well. When I left college, I wasn't 100% sure what was next. I wanted to gain that knowledge, but I didn't know what my path was going to be for sure.

I think that taking time away to reflect and find out what was important to me and what was going to drive me day in and day out was important. I had to think, "If I lost everything today, what would get me up the next morning to go after it?" I spent a great deal of time, especially when I was in Florida, trying to figure those things out, and I think that catapulted me to where I am today.

You mentioned that when you were in Florida, you made the decision to reflect and to actually create a plan and have everything you do to catapult you towards your plan. Why is reflecting and planning so important?

Erica Smith: I wholeheartedly believe in taking the time to always reflect. I try and do it daily, but there's also times where you have to go with the flow. Life happens very fast, and we have to take time away and be purposed and sit down and think, "Where have I been and where am I trying to go? What am I doing right now to get me there?"

I took the time to make sure that I had alignment. You could be doing very well at something, and still not feel successful and still not feel like you're doing what you're supposed to be doing. I took that time to think because I love Sherwin-Williams. I think it's a great company, but at the end of the day, I still had that feeling of, "I should be doing something else, I should be doing more." Taking that time and really figuring out what was important to me, who I wanted to be and how I wanted to live my life; that was the stepping stones of getting me here today.

After Sherwin-Williams, how did you know it was time to step out and become an entrepreneur?

Erica Smith: I came here and took a position with Sherwin-Williams and did that for about a year. With Randstad, one of their recruiters contacted me about taking a position with them. At that point, I was ready to leave Sherwin-Williams, and in my mind, I knew that I probably should've leaped in.

I probably should've stepped out on faith and go towards doing my own thing, but it's hard. It's hard to leave the wheel, right? It's hard to leave the expectation that you're supposed to have a nine to five, or whatever, and supposed to have a steady paycheck. I went and took the position with Randstad, and again, another phenomenal company. I learned a lot of great things there. Learned a lot of different sales techniques. Learned a lot of different management techniques, because we were dealing with people in the workforce.

That position taught me a lot, but last year, I got to that point where I was tired of not being able to do what I wanted to do. I spoke about my mom being sick earlier, and she still deals with a few medical things, and I think that there was a point last year where I was having to make too many choices of, "Am I going to be at her doctor's appointment or am I going to work this thirteen, fourteen hour day and find out on the back end what's going on?" Again, just finding out what's important to me.

If I lost everything last year, would that job have been the most important thing to me? Or, would it have been the time that I was able to spend with my mother and the time that I was able to make sure that I knew the things that I value? That was enough for me to step away and just say, "You know what? These are the things that are important to me, and these are the things that I'm going to invest my time in."

What are some challenges that you face as you've made different career choices?

Erica Smith: I think one of the biggest challenges that I faced was obviously just walking away, or actually having the comfort of, "You're making a nice amount of money." You know that that check's coming in, so you've created a certain type of lifestyle, and you're accustomed to that. The challenge to myself, I guess, after I did that was to not change my lifestyle but make sure that I'm doing the things that I need to do that I could still live that way.

Incorporating different streams of income, making sure that I was always working. For me, working a lot didn't really change, but what changed is that I was working on things that I loved, and so it doesn't feel like work. It doesn't feel like I just worked a fifteen hour day. I'm up at 5am and I'm not in bed until midnight the next day. It doesn't feel like I've been working all day. I've been doing things that I love.

Then another challenge is when you step out own your own, it's always knowing what to do that day. I've done a lot of to-do lists and daily plans, but some days, you don't know what to do next. Earlier, we talked about making sure that you're asking the right questions. I think that that helps a lot—just always having great mentors around you, and reaching out to people to find out more knowledge about the things that you're doing right now.

Who are some people who've opened doors for you that maybe you didn't even know existed, and maybe you could've never gone through on your own?

Erica Smith: I've had a phenomenal core of mentors that have poured into my life and just starting back at SIU, one of my mentors just retired from the College of Business, Michael Haywood. He gave me the opportunity every summer to run a program called Exploring Careers in Business for him from my freshman year in college. The autonomy that he gave me with that, and the ability to pour into young people lives and help them figure out their path has been tremendous. I can't thank him enough for that opportunity because it has prepared me definitely for the things that I'm trying to do today.

Everything that I'm doing is working with young people, and helping them to be successful in everything that they want to do in life. We talk about that. We talk about the mentors that I have with Machine Elite.

Our founders, Harry Dunn and Yomi Martin, the wealth of knowledge that you get from those two guys is unreal. Both have been entrepreneurs for years, so they've seen a lot of different things that you or I probably never would expect, but the wealth of knowledge that they have. The head bumps that I don't have to go through because they've already been there. It's phenomenal. I can't thank them enough for what they've poured into me.

What are the values of Machine Elite?

Erica Smith: Myself and my two business partners took over Machine Elite at the top of this year. The organization has second grade all the way through high school, boys and girls. We focus on not only developing them on the court but off the court. I think some of our greatest accomplishments, and some of the greatest compliments that we receive from parents are the confidence that we've instilled in their kids, and that carries off the basketball court.

We're always talking to them about being leaders. Our Machine Law is no excuses, work hard, and never give up. If you can set your mind to doing those three things every day, you can be successful in anything that you want to do. No excuses, work hard, and never give up.

How can athletes continue to learn and gain coaching when they finish playing sports?

Erica Smith: I think one of the biggest things we forget sometimes is to ask for help because we're so used to doing everything ourselves. We're workaholics, so we forget to ask for help. I've always been a learner, so I've always been like, "How did you do this? Why did you do this?" Just taking from it what's valuable to me, because everybody's going to give you a lot of information, but you just have to learn how to take what's valuable for you at that time.

I think making sure that student-athletes, as they transition, that they're asking a lot of questions, that they're not afraid to say, "I don't know. I've never been here before. How do I get here? What steps should I take?" With that information, they can figure out the best path for them.

More specifically, how can female college athletes transition better?

Erica Smith: The skill sets that we develop as athletes are invaluable. You can take them anywhere and you can do anything with them. I think that a lot of times we forget that and we're like, "Okay, I'm not an athlete anymore, so I'm taking a step back from that aggressive nature that I had, or the never give up, the go after what I want type of mentality," because we're not in sport anymore.

We're not as competitive anymore, but the workforce is competitive. If you want it you have to go get it. The motto that I live by is, "You set the stage that you want to perform on." You have to go get it if you want it, and you have to build up the life that you want.

How do you personally de-stress?

Erica Smith: Believe it or not, I'm not the type of person that stresses alot. People laugh at that, but I made up in my mind a few years back that if I'm stressing over something, it's because I'm letting it control me, and I haven't controlled the situation.

Absolutely, I get overwhelmed, without a doubt. I have a million different things going on, so when I feel that feeling of being overwhelmed, I take a step back and I create a plan. I have X, Y, and Z going on right now, and they're all important.

I sit down and I create a plan to knock off each thing, because when your life is in order, you're not stressed, so I just create a plan to not be stressed—to make sure that I accomplish the things that I need to accomplish, and that I do it in a timely fashion.

That may entail some long days and long nights, but you get the job done and you don't live with that stress of, "I have to do this. I have to do that. I have to do this. I have to do that." Creating that plan has definitely been beneficial to me, but in saying that, I know that I give a lot of myself in anything that I'm doing, so having those positive relationships around me, with friends or family, that you can laugh and you can joke with gives that energy back to you. That's huge for me.

Energy is transferable. You're around successful people, you're around energetic people, you're around happy people, you're around go-getters, that transfers to you. I try and keep those people around me.

What are the final pieces of advice you would like to share with current female student-athletes?

Erica Smith: I've said it probably a million times, "Find out what's important to you." Do it now, while you're in college. Take that time. I know that you're in the experience and you're playing the game right now, and you have this test and you have everything that seems immediate right now.

College is four years, five years for some people, but it's four years of your life. Enjoy the college experience, it's one of the greatest times of your life, but take some time for yourself and really find out what you like to do, and what's important to you. I'm not talking about just title stuff.

We talked about that earlier, of just wanting to be CEO or wanting to be a marketing director or wanting to be a financial advisor, but really take the time to find out what's important to you. Decide the type of life that you want to live, and then create a plan from there.

These are the things that are important to me, and how am I going to get there? How am I going to make sure that in whatever I do, these things stay important to me? I think that that's huge.

Then just keeping that mentality of a student-athlete when you leave, that you're going to obviously juggle a million different things in life, but continue to be accountable. I think that's the biggest thing. I've never met a successful person that isn't accountable.

Whether it's that they're accountable themselves or they have people around them that hold them accountable, accountability is the key to success. Making sure that you stay accountable, you stay aggressive, and you stay resilient, I think that you can achieve whatever you want to.

Erica Smith's Contact Information:
Email: erica@secondwindent.com
Website: www.machineelite.com
Website: www.secondwindent.com
Facebook: Erica Smith
Facebook: Machine Elite Basketball Academy
Facebook: Second Wind Ent
Twitter: @secondwindent22
Instagram: secondwindent22

Chapter 13: PRISCILLA PACHECO TALLMAN

Current occupation: Volleyball Coach and writer.

What college did you attend and what sport did you play?

Priscilla Pacheco Tallman: I played volleyball at the University of Georgia.

How did you decide to attend the University of Georgia? What was the recruiting process like for you?

Priscilla Pacheco Tallman: I really loved the experience prior to it. I had actually gone to some camps. Some of the camps I went to in high school had several college coaches there, so it was a really neat and a unique opportunity to get recruited by many different schools.

One of the coaches that were at one of these camps actually ended up recruiting me for the University of Georgia. I had already known that the setter from that same exact camp and a blocker from that camp were already heading to Georgia. They were people I was very interested in playing with. I had been coached by one of their coaches at the camp so I already knew his style.

I was very attracted to a lot of the things about Georgia, but when I stepped on campus, I knew that was it. Athens is a really, really cool town. The north campus at the University of Georgia is just beautiful, from the architecture to everything and you cannot beat the football.

What was your major and how did you select that major?

Priscilla Pacheco Tallman: I have an undergraduate degree in Psychology and then I have a Master's in Clinical Psychology. It's funny because when I graduated from high school, I really wanted to be in sports psychology. I ended up just wanting to coach. I was very interested intuitively as a senior graduating high school because I knew that here were some things that athletes struggle with and I was really on a quest to find out why and if I could help out other people.

How did you use that immediately when you finished school? How were you able to transition that into your career?

Priscilla Pacheco Tallman: Well, an undergraduate degree in Psychology is very difficult to use in the psychology field. For years, I had a really hard time trying to find work that was fulfilling and that I liked. I ended up as a volunteer assistant coach at Long Beach State University and as a volunteer assistant, you don't get paid anything.

You have to supplement your income to have enough money to live on, so I was working at a bagel shop. I'd go to the bagel shop at 4:30am, we'd open up and I was out at 1:00pm so I could get back to my volunteer coaching job. I had to be at practice by 3pm. I didn't use my degree right away, but I actually found my way into better-paying jobs that were not in psychology.

What has been your career progression?

Priscilla Pacheco Tallman: As athletes, we do the thing that is in front of us. I think that is one of our best assets. We say okay, I don't know the long-term of this, but I do know it's what's right here, so I've got it figured out. Rent is right here, and I've got to figure that out. After the volunteer coaching, I really did need to make money for rent, bills, and that kind of thing.

What worked for me was getting hooked up with a temp agency. I really found success there. I didn't have a professional network. When you're in college, the network you have really is kind of given to you. You don't go in there and learn how to hustle and build that. You have access to tutors and dining halls. You register for your classes first and you have academic advisors. You have a network of people that are there ready to help you succeed.

When you graduate, that process is up to you. You have to figure out your own network. I had a hard time doing that, so I think getting into a temp agency was really helpful for me and for my personality because that was my network. If I could get someone to get me to the job and an interview, I knew I could do well. I knew I could work hard. That was my first step and I ended up being in the corporate world. I was in the internet start-up business for a while. Then I moved into commercial real estate, and land development planning.

I was mostly a project manager and really enjoyed managing projects. That was kind of my thing. Then after 10 years in the corporate world, I decided to go back to grad school. From there I thought I was going to be the sports psychologist that I always wanted to be. After about six years of both grad school and trying to get my licensure hours, I realized private practice was not for me, so I decided to raise my family.

Now, I'm a freelance writer and I raise my kids. I am going to be coaching a little bit more as well. I just really want to reproduce the love of sport that I have in other people. That's where I'm at.

You mentioned that you went to a temp agency. Why did you make that decision?

Priscilla Pacheco Tallman: You know, for me, it might not appear that way now, but I'm actually kind of an introvert. Those networking environments where I have to go and strike up conversations don't appeal to me. I think at that monster.com and newspaper ads were the way people found jobs. The prospect of having to go and do all of that myself was overwhelming.

Somebody told me, "Hey, you should check out a temp agency. They get you into places." For me, that worked because it suited my personality. Again, I'm a logical person and knew I could just get in front of somebody to do an interview—I knew I could interview well. I knew I could do the work when I'm in, so that's why I chose the temp agency.

How did you decide to go from one job to the next, or whether to stay in the city that you live in or to move? How did you make those decisions? What were the criteria?

Priscilla Pacheco Tallman: A lot of things now, for me, are about fulfillment. I make a lot of decisions based on: "Where is this going to fulfill these really deep needs that I have?" Basically, I think about what I want to leave behind. That's where I'm at now in my life. I think earlier in my 20s it was a little bit different. How I made decisions was based on things like, "How much money was I going to make?" and "Can I pay my bills?" It's changed for me.

When you transitioned from playing sports, was work or personal life more challenging and why?

Priscilla Pacheco Tallman: With work, not so much. I think in all of my jobs, I really did what I had to do. The really big bomb was more in my family life. When I had my son, I struggled with postpartum depression.

I had to actually reach out, broaden my circle and ask for help of saying, "I'm embarrassed. I fell. I don't know what to do here." That time in my life was very pivotal for me because as an athlete who had achieved some success and had played at a high level, I honestly did not think post partied depression was possible for somebody like me.

I simply thought that's not going to happen to me. I've done all this stuff as an athlete and that doesn't happen to people like me. It was very important during that time for my husband and I to ask for help. I felt like it wasn't necessarily where we bottomed out, but it was one of those places where I was like, "Wow, that changed a lot of things for us."

I hope that the female college athletes who are reading understand the significance and importance of that because it will save some potential stress. Other people can come up with those solutions that maybe we just hadn't thought of because we're so stuck in our own minds.

What are some ways that you actually de-stress or have de-stressed in the past?

Priscilla Pacheco Tallman: I can de-stress at the gym. I do cross fit. I need the time of just working out and going and doing that. Because I am kind of an introvert, I still really enjoy being in a place that's very quiet and reading a book. Having that time where I'm mindlessly walking around, looking at stuff. Things like that, I really enjoy.

When did you realize that you needed to de-stress?

Priscilla Pacheco Tallman: It took a while actually. Probably at some point after I had children. It's always loud. I think your built in moments are very quiet, so there's always some moments where I could have gotten away, just myself. Once you start adding people into your space, you've got to figure that out.

How have you dealt with conflict in your professional life?

Priscilla Pacheco Tallman: Again, I think that's something that evolves with different stages in our lives and jobs that we have. I was definitely more of a people pleaser kind of person in my earlier jobs and career choices. I said a lot of "okay, yes how can I help you?" It stems from being a player who is used to being coached, so when you come out of college, you have that player mentality of "okay yes, what's the next thing?"

Now, I really have figured out how to go directly to the source. If there's conflict, I ask questions to find a solution such as "Can we talk about this? I'm wondering if you are feeling this or if I'm feeling this? How can we make this work better? What do you bring to the table?

How can I bring something to the table? How can we make that work the best?"

How did dealing with conflict as a college athlete help prepare you to deal with conflict in the professional world?

Priscilla Pacheco Tallman: I found that when we were on the court, it didn't really matter what our conflict was. You know, you're not going to like everybody. You're not going to get along with everybody all the time. What we have to really realize is the importance of managing all of that once we are assigned our projects.

With work, you have a project and you have to determine the goal. From there, you establish how you're going to work together and what the team is going to do together to move forward. I think that was important as well.

It's funny because I talked to some of my friends who I played with in college. Whatever conflict we had back then, it doesn't really matter. We went through something together, so we're good. At the time you think it's so much bigger. I really do attribute a lot of the success we had to our ability to bring it together when we were on the court. We didn't really think about all of that emotional stuff that's off the court so we could focus on our task and just to get it done.

Handling conflict, as you mentioned, is really important in the workplace. What other skills would you say are essential? Maybe some things that are tangible skills that you would say young women need to know?

Priscilla Pacheco Tallman: I would say, I really believe connection is really one of the biggest things that we have as an asset. Staying connected to people we can use as resources. Asking for help, I still think this is a huge piece of this. Not being afraid to go to whoever your supervisor is, or your mentor and say, "Hey, I want clarification on this." So I'd say asking for help, staying connected. Trusting your instinct is huge. That has guided me for a while—trusting my instinct.

How important is the ability to write well as student athletes enter different organizations?

Priscilla Pacheco Tallman: Wow. I think it's very important. Even the way we communicate through social media, structuring a post is important, especially if you're going to use your social media as a platform for employment. How we present ourselves there is important, from the way that we speak to the type of things that we say. That is a very big skill that I'm glad I've been able to develop over time.

Even now, we have so much we can put on social media, like a LinkedIn or any of those networks where you can post an article about something that you're passionate about. You can put your job, your resume, basically, everything is there. When someone comes through there and sees that, they see someone who can communicate well and can write well; it's a great skill.

Is there anything else that you wish you would have known when you were in college that you know now?

Priscilla Pacheco Tallman: When I finished playing, I really, really wish I had used my influence back then for what I'm using it for now. I know some of that comes with age, but when I played, my mindset was "Oh it's me and look at how great this is." You get awards, but I really wish I had used my influence for other people.

Serving, volunteering, getting plugged in with a mentor group, coaching young teens, all that kind of stuff. I did a little bit of that, but again, I was really career focused from the beginning. I really wish I had known how to use that when I was in my 20's. I think that would have been something that would have been very fulfilling to me, but I think that was one of the missing pieces during that time.

It is so fulfilling to give that back, to serve, and have that "Oh wow they thought that was cool" moment. I think it's one of those pieces that is a really great thing to develop just for life.

What are the final pieces of advice you would like to share with current female student-athletes?

Priscilla Pacheco Tallman: Your ability to rise from a mistake is indicative of how successful you will be. Even as an athlete, you're making mistakes while you are playing. Also, it's not always just pulling yourself up from your bootstraps. A lot of the time, it is asking for help.

That is not a character trait that athletes like to do. We do not like to ask for help and tell people what we need. That has been the important for me as I've gotten older because I can find success after I had made a mistake. My advice to female college athletes is to ask for help and keep going.

Priscilla Pacheo Tallman Contact Information:
Email: pytallman@gmail.com
Facebook: Priscilla Pacheco Tallman
Twitter: @pytallman
Instagram: pytallman

Chapter 14: CECELIA TOWNES

Current occupation: Attorney, blogger, and speaker.

Where did you attend college and what sport did you play?

Cecelia Townes: I played tennis at Howard University. I played all four years that I was there. I was the team captain for my last year. It was a great experience. Howard's D1; it's in the MEACC conference.

What was your greatest accomplishment during your athletic career?

Cecelia Townes: Aside from any wins, my greatest accomplishment was being a leader and being a mentor to the girls who were younger than me. Especially the girls who were two and three years younger than me, we were able to form a genuine sisterhood. I was able to offer them guidance and support. That still carries on today. That's probably my biggest accomplishment—developing into a leader, and learning to be a better friend and teammate.

What did you major in, and why did yo select this major?

Cecelia Townes: I was an African-American Studies major and a History minor. Initially, I started off in Biology because I was going to be a doctor. I chose African-American Studies because I just fell in love with the subject matter and I fell in love with the people that I was learning about. People who are advocating for other people.

I didn't know exactly that I wanted to go to law school at that time when I changed my major, but I knew that the labs weren't it for me. I knew that medical school wasn't where I wanted to be. I knew that I wanted to study something that I was interested in.

What motivated you to attend law school?

Cecelia Townes: It all really goes back to advocating for other people. Like I said, part of the reason why I fell in love with African-American Studies was the people that I was reading about, and learning about. That was what I wanted to do. I wanted to just figure out a way to fight for disenfranchised people or people just who weren't heard.

In my senior year, I actually made the decision. I was like, "The best way to do it, for me, is to go to law school." I initially thought that I was going to do international human rights law, then criminal law and certain things didn't pan out. That's what set me on a path to law school. I wanted to help other people and advocate for the people.

How does a young athlete make a decision about which career path to choose?

Cecelia Townes: I was talking to a group of students at Clayton State recently. What I was telling them is that you have to find what you're passionate about and you also have to find what you're good at. If you want to help people, there're a million and one ways to help people, but you should really be trying to help people the way that best fits your skill set and your passion.

How did you go about securing your first job?

Cecelia Townes: It was really networking based on who I knew. I went straight from undergrad to law school. I graduated in 2006 from undergrad, and 2009 from law school. I was in the thick of the economic recession. It was very difficult to find a job, and basically, a friend of the family knew someone in an office in DC. In the Office of Campaign Finance, to be exact, and they gave me a chance. That summer, I needed to stay for the bar exam, so they were gracious enough to let me study and work part-time. When I passed the bar, I came on full-time.

How did they know that you were looking?

Cecelia Townes: I was telling everybody I knew I needed a job. One of the things that I would take to my grave and pass on to my children, and my children's children, that I got from my grandmother is, "A closed mouth don't get fed." If you don't speak up, ask, say what you want, and say what you need, nobody's going to be there to help you.

What were some challenges you may have faced as you were going through your different career choices?

Cecelia Townes: Definitely for me, at that time, was the job market. When I was in law school, I was very criminal defense oriented, so I wanted to specifically work for a criminal defense firm, or work for a public defender's office. When I came out, agencies were having hiring freezes, firms were firing people, so the job market was very, very contracted. That was a challenge. The other challenge is, really just setting yourself apart because whether the economy is good or not, the market is often saturated with people who are trying to do the same thing. That was a challenge, too. Setting myself apart and really learning to play up my skill set became increasingly important. Learning the art of connecting with people and networking with people was a bit of a challenge.

What's a mistake that you've made and how did you handle the situation?

Cecelia Townes: First, my mindset is simply that I'm going to fix it and I'm going to learn it, but that doesn't mean that I don't make mistakes. I have a really good example. A few years ago, I was at work and I had this really big case. The way my job works is, I deal with my clients, but then I also deal with DOJ (Department of Justice). When we're working in litigation, the DOJ talks to the court, I talk to DOJ and then I talk to my clients.

I'm basically a liaison between my client and DOJ. Usually, when things have to get submitted to the court, I type up a draft and then I give it to the DOJ attorney. He or she edits it the way they want it, and then they send it off. This one time, he changed it. I was changed before it got submitted. When it finally got submitted, he completely took out something that was absolutely important to the case. We ended up losing, and part of the reason that we lost was because what I originally put in there wasn't there. This was probably one of the biggest cases that I have had since I've been an attorney.

What I learned from that was the importance of speaking up and being very intentional, and being very clear with people. At the end of the day, even though DOJ is submitting their information, I always have to protect my client. It's my job to make sure that whatever somebody submits on their behalf, or whatever somebody does on behalf of my client, it's a 110% to my approval.

Since it was already submitted, it was a little late to change things. My bosses and supervisors were trying to blame me. I had to really provide proof that what I submitted was completely different, and in a lot of ways, it was out of my control. I explained what happened and I stood up for myself, absolutely. In office settings, there's often a lot of politics. I had to make sure I stood up for myself, and I just let people know it wouldn't happen again.

You bring up a really good point about office politics. When you don't agree with the morals, ethics or policies in your work environment, how do you handle that? You're a lawyer, so I'm sure there a lot of grey area at times.

Cecelia Townes: It depends. As an attorney, I have a lot of moving parts. Sometimes, there's a situation where I don't agree with what a client is doing. I don't agree with it because it's bad policy or it's breaking the law. It's not only something that I would want to tell them to stop doing, or change what we're doing, but I have an obligation to tell them. I do that on that end. As far as working with my peers and my co-workers, a lot of times, it just involves being tactful.

There was an instance, not too long ago in my office, where I didn't agree with the way something was handled. My style of doing it is just to approach people directly, but professionally. There's no need to be childish about things, but when you see something's wrong, you do have to speak up. In a lot of job settings, the vast majority of job settings, if you speak up against something that's illegal and you get fired for it, that's against the law, anyway. You have a level of protection in that regard.

Also, one of the things that I do is employment law. I think that a lot of times, it helps to take your problems to someone else in the organization and not directly to a co-worker. Let's say, you have a problem with a co-worker or you have a problem with your boss, it's not always easy or efficient to go directly to that person. Going through Human Resources, telling them your side and actually having them mediate for you is often very helpful as well.

What are some examples of ways that you've used what you've learned in sports in your day-to-day life?

Cecelia Townes: I would definitely say, even though my main sport was tennis, I also ran track since the 7th grade. Those are individual sports, but they're also very team-oriented. I learned to work with people, and to collaborate, and to mediate between teammates. The leadership is something that I learned. From my experience, dealing with my own teammates, even if they're athletes who aren't necessarily the team captain, they are able to develop a sense of leadership. That's one of the biggest things that I've learned from being an athlete.

What does it take to be a good leader?

Cecelia Townes: I think it takes listening. I think it takes being patient. I also think it takes being creative. What I mean by creative is being able to get what you want from people in different ways. Understanding that not everybody responds the same way to the same thing. If you look at coaches, there are some coaches whose style is to yell and scream. You've got half of them that's going to light a fire, and the other half is looking at you crazy. I think that to be a good leader, you have to be able to inspire people in different ways to get them to move as a unit.

What, from your professional experience, are the most transferable skills for attempting to adapt in this current market?

Cecelia Townes: In the current market, one of the things that I hear that's really important to a lot of companies, and these are private companies and government agencies, is this idea of diversity. Something that I learned from sports was to be able to deal with different races, different personality types, just different backgrounds. I find that athletes, usually, are a lot more open to dealing with different groups of people, because they've been doing it for so long.

Being able to work in a diverse environment is absolutely something that is important in today's market. Being flexible is also important in today's market. I feel like so many agencies, so many companies, especially with the tech companies, are in transition and they're always changing. You have to be able to adapt. That's the same thing you do with sports. You are adapting to the situation every second, every minute of playing time and practice time.

Will you talk a little bit about what you're doing in addition to being an attorney?

Cecelia Townes: I have two big things on my plate right now. One is my blog, it's called Gladiators.com, and we focus on women's sports and issues that involve women in sports. We highlight different athletes. We highlight people who are married to athletes. We highlight sexism in sports, racism in sports. Everything that could deal with women in sports, we talk about.

The other big project that I have, and I'm really excited about, is my company, Beyond The Game. Our main goal is to empower student athletes by giving them workshops to help them with life skills. Our workshops focus on student-athletes' rights and student-athlete wellness. We focus on financial literacy. We focus on personal branding and professional development. Our goal is to help bridge the gap between what they get in the classroom, what they get in the sports and what they need in their life.

How do you balance being an attorney, having a business, and a blog all?

Cecelia Townes: I had to realize that my calendar is literally my best friend now. If I lose that calendar or if I don't set something up to ping me, to remind me, there's no way that I would keep up. I'm constantly filling up and checking my calendar. I balance it that way. Also, I have to remind myself to take it one day at a time, because it gets very frustrating when you try to think too far in advance. There's so much on the calendar. There's so much that you want to do that it will get frustrating if you don't take it one day at a time.

With all that you have going on, how do you de-stress?

Cecelia Townes: Working out because once an athlete, always an athlete. I guess I didn't realize it as much when I was playing sports because you're doing it to be competitive. Now, if I have a hard day at work, or my mind just can't get clear, I really have to go run. You have to go work out. That's the biggest thing for me.

What are the final pieces of advice you would like to share with current female student-athletes?

Cecelia Townes: Honestly, it goes back to what we were talking about earlier, which is finding your purpose. I would hope that women would start focusing on what they like with sincerity and passion. What would you do for free? Figure out, how you are going to make a living off of that passion. Then, pursue that until the end. Don't stop. Once you find it, you go for it.

When you find your purpose, that's something that nobody else can fulfill the same way you can. There will be a space for you in this world to do what you want to do and you make the space. Kick open the doors!

Cecelia Townes Contact Information:
Email: cecelia@livebeyondthegame.com
Facebook: Cecelia Townes
Twitter:@sportyesquire
Instagram: sportyesquire
Website: ceceliatownes.com

Chapter 15: CLAIRE ZOVKO

Current Occupation: *Entrepreneur, Attorney, Professor and founder of Sports Law Chat.*

Where did you attend college and what sport did you play?

Claire Zovko: I played basketball at Pacific Lutheran University.

What was your major in undergrad and why did you select that major?

Claire Zovko: Sure. Back when I was at Pacific Lutheran, I studied Business Administration. My reason for choosing that was, at that time when I was 18 years old, I really didn't know what I wanted to do. I didn't know what the future held because my focus was just pretty much on basketball at that point. What I did was I looked at: "What degree would give me the most options available? What degree would prepare me the most for life?" Since I wasn't drawn to a specific path as an 18-year-old, I said, "Let me pick a path that's just going to open a lot of doors." That's why I chose Business Administration—because I realized whether I work for a business or maybe one day have my own business, these are tangible, valuable skills that are going to help me in life no matter what.

What are some of the challenges female athletes face as they transition from playing sports?

Claire Zovko: Sure. Thinking back, everything was always planned out. You knew in high school what you were going to do next. You knew once you went to college. You picked a degree and you were studying that. You kind of had a path laid out to get that degree. I remember when the ball stopped bouncing per se and basketball was over, I came into this space where it was, "What's next?" It was a space of unknown. I didn't know what I was going to do because I defined myself as a basketball player for so long. There was this uneasiness.

In my case, I always loved school. I knew I was going to go back to school. It was just a matter of deciding what. I was looking at law school and business school. Then again, when I ended up choosing law school and when I finished law school, the same thing happened. "Now that law school's over, what is next? How am I going to use this? Where am I going to go?" Just this space of unknown, which can be very scary. I remember that.

Also, from working with professional athletes now, some of my clients that are recent athletes, WNBA players, and others, they talk about the same thing. Once the WNBA's over, they're in the space of figuring out what to do, what they are good at and how to add value to in a professional environment.

From my journey, the way I got clarity was just to answer the questions, "What do I truly have a passion about? I might like many things, but what comes easily to me?" In my case, I love learning and I conversely love teaching. Teaching does come naturally to me. I looked for opportunities, once I was done, to teach. I got that in the college environment and in the sports business environment.

Then also I got that in the yoga environment because really it's a skill set. Whether I'm teaching college students about the Globalization of Sport or I'm teaching the principles of yoga to the community, it's the skill set of teaching that again, anywhere I go in my life, that teaching skill set can and will apply. Just think about those skill sets that you already embody and come naturally to you.

How did you realize that teaching was your skill set?

Claire Zovko: I didn't, at first, probably, but it was from some conversations with people. Then I looked back on my life. My mother is a teacher. I had this small, limited view that when I say teacher, I mean like an elementary school teacher. Since she was that, for some reason, I had this resistance and said, "That's not what I want to be. I don't want to be a teacher because it somehow reminded me of that. I didn't see myself as an elementary school teacher.

I had such a limited view until my eyes opened. I didn't realize that teaching is millions of things. It's this really broad definition. My mom pointed out to me; she's like, "Claire, look. Do you realize that you've been tutoring your friends your whole life?" Math came easy for me, but not for others.

I love having a problem. If someone doesn't understand it, it's my lack of communication if I can't explain in a new way to help someone understand something I understand. That's a challenge I like. That's why I'd tutor or support or help my friends because I wanted to show them that math can be easy. You just have to communicate it in a way that speaks to that particular student or person. My mom brought that up. "You've basically been teaching people your whole life." It hit me. I said, "Yeah, that's right." Not that I was ever in a professor-student environment up until the point, but I look back on the things that I'd done and I've been teaching my whole life.

What were some challenges that you faced when you transitioned from college in securing your first job?

Claire Zovko: In between undergrad and law school, I took 2 years off. I saw that basketball and sports were coming to an end. I did make the transition to the professional world. I still had this desire to be involved in sports because it did provide this environment that I feel like created the foundation of who I am today. I couldn't let it go right away. Even when I was in school my last couple years before it was over, I started volunteering and working with the Seattle Sonics and Seattle Reign at that time. The NBA team and then the ABL team that was in Seattle at that time before the Seattle Storm came. I just got involved. I just wanted to be there and get involved.

Then it progressed. I started out passing out bobble heads at the door. I started out doing time out promotions, just anything to be there. It continued to grow. I continued to meet people in the organization. When I finished school, I was able to take a more prominent role with the team and worked in investor relations.

Then, by the time I knew I was going to law school, I saw the attorney of the team at the games. We definitely knew each other by face, but we never had a full conversation. I intentionally went out of my way to have a sit down with him and have an informal interview before I left and just plant the seed that, "Hey, now he knows who I am and

I'm going to law school and I'm interested in keeping in contact with you."

I learned about his daily responsibilities and started to bridge that relationship. When I went to law school, I continued to keep in touch with him periodically. Fast forward, that ended up being my internship. Between my second and third year of law school, I started to work with the Seattle SuperSonics within legal and basketball operations. When I graduated law school, that ended up being my job.

For me, it was not an abrupt transition once I was finished. I wanted to continue to plant seeds along the way and cultivate them to create the professional opportunity I wanted. At that time, it was my dream job. It wasn't work and wasn't a stress either. It was fun, enlightening. I was learning every single day in the sport I love on the professional side.

You mentioned that "That was my dream job at the time." It's important to note that because we go through changes. When did you realize that it was time to make another move from Seattle to Miami?

Claire Zovko: What I realized was that I'd stayed local for undergrad. It wasn't far from where I grew up. When I had the opportunity to go to law school and transition to another city, I knew it was my chance. I knew, "Here's the reason I can go live in another city and, when it's over, I can always come back home. Home doesn't go anywhere." I knew it was just time.

I felt there was more that, by getting out, there was more growth available to me. That's what I wanted. I looked at law schools in southern California and south Florida. The University of Miami worked out and everything aligned for that opportunity.

I say it's the best decision I ever made because it broke me out of the box and I realized again there's more than what I had in my little box of the world. I totally believe that being at Miami in law school is why I got the Sonics job. At the time, they were getting hundreds of resumes to be a summer intern every year, but I was someone different because I wasn't at the local law schools where everyone else who applied was from the two local law schools.

There was nothing different about them. I was the Seattle girl that went to Miami and had this other experience. I truly believe that's why I stood out from the pack and even got in that situation.

Then again, by getting out, my worldview grew. Miami is one of the most international cities. I almost feel like I'm in a foreign country down here. I love it. That has just continued to make me grow. For work, I got to go to Brazil and work with some companies down there related to preparing to go for the Olympics about five or six years ago.

I've had all kinds of different travel opportunities, which again just continue to broaden my worldview. Related to the dream job, that was my dream job at that time. Now I see there's so much more. I was only thinking domestically.

The United States is wonderful, but the United States is really small. On the job front, the whole world is the opportunity and possibility out there. Now I realize that and see that. I can't even define my dream job anymore because I realize if I try to define it, I'm limiting myself. I'm just open. I know it's out there, but I'm continually asking myself, "What value can I provide to who and where can I be of service with the skills, abilities, talents, and passions that I have?

Why are you so passionate about the impact of sports on a global level? How did teaching the course "The Globalization of Sports" come about?

Claire Zovko: It circles back to the experiences that have arisen in my life. I have this desire to travel, meet people, learn, grow and see how other systems work. I guess it all goes back to that love of learning. I had the opportunity when I got out of law school to be a teaching assistant for a study abroad program in Florence, Italy for two summers. The course that was being taught was International Sports Law. I had two summers to be in a foreign country and help teach to law students about international sports law.

That started to turn the wheels for me. I really enjoyed it. Then when I came back to Miami with one of my colleagues, we were able to propose a brand new course at Miami Law called The Olympic Games and the Law. We created that, taught that, and it went well.

After doing all of those two courses for about six semesters, I felt ready I could teach this on my own. However, I wanted to adapt it and make it a little different and not so much focused on the law, but the global business of sport. That doesn't just apply to lawyers but it applies to many people. I proposed a new undergrad course within the Sports Administration program. They loved it.

The Dean said she had been wanting a class like this forever, but she just didn't have time to create it or they didn't have the resources for it. When I showed up, they said, "No problem." This new course gave me the green light to roll with it and create it. I've taught it six or seven semesters now. It keeps evolving. The way I taught it in semester one is different than how I'm going to teach it this fall because global sports keeps evolving. The issues that keep coming up, I can't make them up. They're so interesting. With Rio and the Zika virus, that's an interesting issue that's never been talked about before and the liability related to that.

The beauty of the Globalization of Sport, and with the prevalence of technology, is that globalization of sports is huge but, at the same time, it's very well connected because no matter where you are, you can touch it on some level. I think no matter what area of sport or business you seek to work in, this topic could be relevant. The students seem to find it quite interesting. I really enjoy sharing.

You talked about alignment and how your passion and opportunities began to align and things opened up for you. For the young women who will read this book, could you talk about alignment and how important that is for fulfillment in life?

Claire Zovko: I think that's the key. This one, what I'm about to say, might not make sense or might be against the grain. Here's what has worked for me time and time again: I noticed back in the day when I was applying for jobs, I'd see a job posting and then I would somehow try to convince someone else that I was that person who they were looking for, that perfect candidate. I'd say, "yeah, I'm A, B, C and D."

I realized that was just some sham. It wasn't true. It wasn't an alignment. I actually stopped applying to jobs off postings because I said, "I'm not like this magical person that they're saying they're looking for. It's not me. I'm someone else. I'm unique and have different skills and abilities."

What I started doing is I started thinking about, "What am I good at? How can I add value? How can I make someone else's job easier?" Once I figured that out and had that clarity, then what I would do is tell them. Like I told you a moment ago how I had that opportunity to be a teaching assistant in Italy. That wasn't something that was posted. When I heard that that opportunity was going to happen, I got an email that said, "Hey we're doing a study abroad in Italy." Right away, I knew I needed to be on that trip. That was natural to me. I said, "I have to be on this trip and I'm no longer a student, so I can't be a student, but I want to be involved. I know this is just an amazing thing that can help me evolve and grow and learn."

I wrote an email to the professor, who I did not know at that time, and I said exactly what I just told you. Then I explained the value I could provide and how I could make his time in Italy easier and make his job easier. I offered to be his teaching assistant.

He said, "Wow. That's amazing. It sounds like I just have to show up to class and you do all the work." I said, "Yeah, that's basically it." He wanted to enjoy Italy, so he invited me to come along as his graduate assistant.

That's only one example. I've noticed that for me, it's worked out to truly get into alignment with my skills, abilities, and passions and then not convince, but persuade someone that my presence is going to help them sleep at night. That's going to make their job easier, smoother.

As long as someone has the budget for it, people love that and people want that. There are times when someone says, "I'd love to have you, but I can't pay you or we can't have someone on staff." That's a different case, which has taught me the other lesson that, in situations like that when you do get a no, all that truly means is no, not right now. It doesn't mean no forever.

The same thing with the Sonics opportunity and how I started working with the Sonics. When I got in with the lawyer, I applied after the first summer and didn't get the job, but I still felt this in me that I knew I wanted it and I knew I could add value and I knew it wasn't the end. I wanted to keep pursuing it. I didn't let the no be a closed door. I just said, "Okay, not right now. Continue to cultivate that relationship. Continue to plant seeds." When it came around the next year as an opportunity, then it was successful.

With me, I've noticed if I'm in alignment and as clear as I can be with myself, what's interested in me, what I'm interested in, my skills and passion, it feels natural. It's not a struggle. It's not forced. I'm not worried. If I don't get it, I'm not worried. I know there's something else for me. I had an amazing interview with a current dream job a few months ago. If I got it, it would have been amazing. I didn't get it, but it's okay because that experience, I learned so much. For me, it was part of realizing that I was even considered for that position.

I had this realization of my value and that I was underplaying my value. Once they interviewed me as a candidate I just say, "Wow they're even considering me. I need to step into my own greatness now." Though I didn't get the job, I took away a lot. I'm more in alignment now with who I am. I know that if that door opened, there are some other pretty cool doors around the corner. I'm ready for them. I'm more in alignment as a whole in what I can offer a larger organization at this point.

How are you using what you learned from playing sports over the years in your daily life?

Claire Zovko: One of the biggest lessons I had to learn through sports in high school and in college was realizing I was a part of that team that was on my shirt. Being a part of that meant not only on the court when things are going well, but it also meant when things weren't going well on the court. It was a lesson I had to learn the hard way in high school and college of who I'm representing. Being a part of a team—applies later in life in your work environment or as part of your company—you're representing something larger.

It's important to have that mindfulness that it's not all about you or not all about me or not all about the person. In addition, it's key to be aware of who your client is, aware of who you're working with or working for and having that broader view that everything you do and say and the actions you take don't just impact you. I use that constantly, especially if there's a conflict, whether it's within my work or it's with someone outside of the work. I take some time to pause and think about that "Who am I representing? How can I speak in the interests of who I'm representing, not in the interests of Claire? How can I best represent whoever I'm representing?" As a lawyer, I'm representing people all of the time. It's an important question. It's something that's important to be very clear on. That's a huge one for me that I go back to all the time.

With all that you have going on, how do you de-stress? I know you're avid at yoga and you recently came back from five weeks in India. Will you talk a little bit about that experience and why yoga is such a key part of who you are?

Claire Zovko: The time in India was quite incredible. The other interesting thing about yoga is I started yoga right after basketball finished. If I would have been doing yoga when I was an athlete, it would have been a whole different ballgame. I realize now how disconnected I was from the feelings in my body that I didn't see the connection. We were taught through sports to be very strong, hit the gym, get stronger, and get faster. I felt like there was a gap missing in terms of it's important to get strong and it's also very important and critical to have the matching flexibility to your strength.

Now, through yoga, I've learned that. I've felt that. I've experienced that. Now when I just go play around for fun and go play a pickup game, I feel amazing. The way I move on the court feels so fluid. It's because I've created more of this balance internally within my body through the yoga. For me, now I've been practicing yoga for twelve or thirteen years and the journey just keeps going deeper and deeper. I'd say I'm at a place now where I use yoga and a daily meditation practice to be preventative in the stress.

I get in a clear place, in a stable place, and get in a grounded place daily so that when something triggers me or when something starts to cause stress in the body, I can notice that and watch it and have an inquiry on "Why is this happening? Why is X stressing me out?" Once I realize why X, Y, or Z is stressing me out, I go back even deeper like, "What's that all about? What is that attached to? Where is that coming from?"

The thing is, once you get to the root, you can move through it. You can transcend it. You can get past it. Those same things that triggered me a year ago no longer trigger me. I'm having less stress in my body now than a year ago because I'm trying to consciously be preventative of having stress in my life. For me, it's not "I work hard and then I de-stress." It's "There's no separateness." It's "Showing up from a connected place and realizing when stress is occurring and deciding to let that be a part of me or not be a part of me.

Once you get to the root of it and you find really some root of something that's causing you stress, it's really amazing that as you clear that out, things just open up. They truly open up. Yeah, that's where I'm at. I'm just all about having less stress in my life than needing to de-stress from it later.

How does someone cultivate that skill? I agree, it is important; powerful, graceful, and respectful combined.

Claire Zovko: The triple threat. It's a challenge. I'd say for me it's a matter of trial and error, but knowing that the loudest voice in the room isn't the most powerful. People that can whisper and everyone's totally locked in and focused on them, they have power. What I've learned, too, is that our presence is one of the strongest things we have. When we walk in a room, we actually don't need to speak, but there's a presence that's either felt when you walk in or not. How do you cultivate that? From my experience, what has worked for me and the people that I've been around is getting in your stillness. You have to get still. If we're always going a million miles an hour, there's no clarity. Think about a snow globe. If you shake it up, it's all crazy. You can't even see what's inside. There's just stuff going everywhere. That's us when we're going a million miles an hour.

Then when you pause, when you let the snow globe be still and you set it on the table, all that stuff goes away. Now you have the Taj Mahal or you have whatever's on the inside and it's completely beautiful. That's the same thing with us. We have to stop. We have to pause. We have to breathe. Then in that, we start to feel our own presence. When we walk in a room, we have to stop. We have to pause. We have to breathe.

If I'm thinking, "Here's what I got to say. Here's what I need to respond." That's not going to be clear. That's going to be all crazy. When I can have a connection from the heart to the throat and say, that's going to be clear. That comes from stilling yourself, coming down. Be still.

That stillness and that clarity is not often talked about, definitely not in competitive sports. How do we teach young women to do that?

Claire Zovko: Probably starting with the awareness that just how I talked about when I was playing, no one even told me flexibility was important. People said, "You got to be mentally tough," but I'm not sure if I was really taught how to do that.

Now with the prevalence of these different mindfulness techniques, where you are being mindful of your breath, what you're experiencing, what you're feeling it's helping. I think just awareness and education about the benefits will make a difference. If you look at top athletes of our time such as Michael Jordan and LeBron James, they get still. They pause. They do yoga. They meditate.

You can get into that zone a lot quicker when you have that ability to focus, calm down, pause, stop and breathe. Somehow if it could be relayed to athletes that this is of benefit because a lot of people like we're speaking to and moving to are thinking, "I don't have time to stop. I have too much to do. I got to get in 5,000 shots. I got to do this. I got to do that." Maybe only experience can show this. That kind of awareness can transform athletes lives on and off the court.

What are the final pieces of advice you would like to share with current female student-athletes?

Claire Zovko: I'd say one of the things that I've learned and had a journey with throughout basketball until now is communication and realizing the power of my voice when it's clear and being confident in that, being confident that, as a woman, I do have a voice. I have a valuable opinion. I can add value. Thinking back, I wish I would have been more confident in the things I wanted to say, but also clearer in the things I wanted to say and not afraid to say something different or not afraid to say something against the grain.

That's what I think is beautiful in our world and as women, another beautiful thing is that we do look at things differently, maybe from a more motherly, nurturing, loving perspective. That's what businesses need. If it's just ten men in the room and they're making all the decisions, they're only looking at fifty percent of the picture. As women, we provide this incredible other view that we can share and add value to whatever environment we're in. I would say the value and ability to communicate powerfully, but yet gracefully and respectfully will help female athletes as they transition from college.

Claire Zovko Contact Information:
Email:clairezovko@hotmail.com
Facebook: Claire Zovko
Twitter: @clairezovko

CONCLUSION

Throughout the book, you've read a number of experiences from dynamic women who are all former collegiate athletes pursuing their goals. They come from different parts of the world but they have consistent experiences. Some of you may have read this book looking for a step by step process to achieving your goals.

However, there is one consistent theme to each person's experience— there isn't a straight path to success. Despite the desire to have the blueprint, your personality, past experiences, and commitment determine the outcomes. Similar to playing sports at a high level, if you are to have a high-level career, you will need the right coaching, strategy, and ability to overcome the obstacles.

Osa Osula finished her eligibility at George Mason University and decided to go to Europe for a pro combine in an effort to get signed. A team from Germany saw her, asked her to tryout, but she didn't make the team. Consequently, the team did not buy her another flight back to New York, so she was stranded in Germany without many of the necessities. Her plan was uprooted, but she utilized her resources and ended up making a different team while taking independent studies courses.

Similarly, Emily Jaskowiak would have never considered herself a runner while playing college basketball at the University of Tulsa, but she decided to train for a 50-mile ultra marathon. She pushed herself to the limits and had an emotional breakdown during one of her training runs. After regaining her composure, she kept going and ultimately completed the race! Emily explained she learned so much about her ability to overcome obstacles.

In this book, many of the women discussed how their love for the game and why they are eager to continue to be a resource for other young women who are approaching the transition to the workforce. Similarly, I will never forget growing up playing basketball with my brothers in the backyard at our house in the hot humid St. Louis summers. As my commitment to the game grew, so did my self-esteem and confidence.

Ultimately, I earned a full athletic scholarship to play basketball at St. Louis University and then continued on to play in Germany. Although I played in Germany, I didn't prepare well for life after college and realized that many athletes graduate without a clear understanding of the next steps to take in their professional careers.

After playing, I began the journey of finding a career that I loved. This led to coaching basketball at the collegiate level, working in public education and eventually launching the Global Athlete Media Network, which provides media services to current and former athletes.

As I reflect on my experiences, there were many disappointments along the way. When the end of my collegiate career approached, I wanted to play professionally, but I didn't have a contract signed, nor did I have a backup plan. I considered being a graduate assistant, but

I hadn't applied to graduate school nor was there a clear understanding of the admissions process.

Consequently, the day of graduation I stood in front of the mirror filled with uncertainty. Similar to the other women in the book, I had to overcome challenges and disappointments that eventually led me down to this moment today.

One of the most nauseating feelings occurs when you have prepared for an opportunity, but things do not go as planned. After my senior season ended at St. Louis University in 2004, I found out there was going to be an exposure event at the Final Four in New Orleans for seniors who wanted to pursue playing basketball professionally.

This event would give a lot of players with hoop dreams the opportunity to show their skills in front of agents and scouts. As soon as I found out about it, I sent in my registration form and payment because I couldn't let this opportunity pass. At the Women's College Basketball Association (WBCA) Convention, I planned to participate in the *So You Want to Be a Coach* program and attend the WBCA banquet to receive the Robin Roberts Sports Communication Award.

Once the convention activities ended, I headed to the combine with a few of my college coaches.

When I arrived, I found out the event organizer changed the start time of the event, so I didn't get a chance to play. I was extremely disappointed, but it was a critical moment to make a decision that would impact the rest of my life. My coaches and I discussed the possibility of playing overseas and they connected me to someone who knew an agent in Germany. We sent the agent my game film and months later, I received a contract to play.

Every time you are presented with a challenge, you have the opportunity to learn a lesson. I could have given up after the incident with the combine, but I would have missed out on the lesson. In this situation, I learned to always call to reconfirm meeting times. If I would have called her the day before, I would have known the time changed. Even though missing the opportunity to play in front of the pro scouts was a tough lesson to learn, I still had to figure out the next steps.

I am thankful to the coaches who were my guides and mentors as I continued to pursue my goal of playing professionally. Once I stopped playing, I decided to attend graduate school full time and begin coaching. Ten years ago, I was an assistant coach at Metro High School in St. Louis with some of the most competitive and brilliant young women I'd ever met. We won a state championship led by a group of seniors who held the team to high standards.

These young women personified poise, grace, and intensity. Recently, I saw one of the young women at the Final Four in Indianapolis; she explained the challenges of being a young professional who is trying to make a career decision. She played college basketball at Morgan State University and entered a coaching career immediately afterwards. As we talked, the frustration in her voice was evident and we discussed some solutions to her situation. This encounter was confirmation that there's a need for guidance and mentors for female athletes.

Over the past decade, I have coached and mentored female student-athletes at multiple universities and institutions. The lack of exposure and access to professionals beyond the university setting is common. However, if young women are given insight to what's possible by learning from others, they can step into future leadership roles with confidence and competence.

Our goal for this book was to assist you with creating the next best step for your life. Trust me you don't have to know exactly what the next twenty years will entail, but we want you to be comfortable with the next step. As you read from the contributors, we are still finding new interests and exploring unexpected opportunities that come our way. Nevertheless, what we know for sure is that having people on your team who have traveled the path you are heading can accelerate your growth.

Anyone who has achieved a significant level of success knows that it doesn't happen alone. Therefore, we want to hear from you and support you as you pursue your goals. Each woman in this book would have loved to have had access to a group of professional mentors who have already committed to providing guidance.

Now the ball is in your court. Take the initiative and reach out to us and ask questions or comments about our experiences. We are here to ensure you don't make the same mistakes we've made. What challenges are you facing? How has playing sports equipped you to manage this situation? What resources do you have available that will allow you to accomplish your goal? As you've read, we are not perfect and none of us pretend like that is our reality. Nevertheless, we come to you authentically and ready to provide coaching for your life beyond playing sports.

ABOUT THE AUTHOR

Angela Lewis is a former professional basketball player, championship winning coach and owner of Global Athlete Media Network which provides successful athletes the media platforms to expand their brands. She is also the recipient of the prestigious Robin Roberts Sports Communication Award.

Basketball became Angela first love, giving her the confidence and work ethic to excel in life. Standing five feet eight inches tall in the fifth grade, she had low self-esteem and was uncomfortable in her own skin. Through practice and commitment, Angela earned a full athletic scholarship to play basketball at St. Louis University. In four years, Angela scored over 1,000 points, grabbed over 500 rebounds while received many awards athletically and academically.

After playing in Germany, she coached at Metro High School, Webster University, and Southeast Missouri State University and served as director of basketball operations at Marquette University. In her last coaching stint with the St. Louis Surge, Angela helped lead the team to a National Championship. While working with numerous athletes over the years, she decided to help them develop beyond the game.

Angela continues to use sports to enhance the lives of youth globally. She facilitated leadership sessions at the Nike Elite 100 Camp, the National Youth Summit on Economics, Justice, and Education, and numerous educational institutions. In addition, she travels globally hosting basketball clinics and conducting leadership training for young women. Her books, *The Game Changing Assist: Six Simple*

Ways to Choose Success and The Game Changing Assist Workbook are used with youth programs throughout the country.

With a love for entrepreneurship and youth, Angela is the Regional Director of Network for Teaching Entrepreneurship's (NFTE) St. Louis. NFTE is a global non-profit which inspires students from underserved communities to start businesses and have the entrepreneurial mindset. In addition to managing corporate partnerships, she provides coaching to help students launch businesses.

As a host on Business Innovators Radio, contributor to Small Business Trendsetters and Business Innovators Magazine she covers influencers, innovators and trendsetters in sports, business and finance. Angela is also the producer and host of the Athletes as Educators podcast.

Angela has been honored by Black Girls Rock St. Louis, and received the Distinguished Young Professional in Education and Youth Empowerment from the Urban League of Metropolitan St. Louis. She is a St. Louis native who holds a B.A. and M.A. in Communication from Saint Louis University.

Angela Lewis' Contact Information:
Email: info@globalathletemedia.com
Facebook: Angie Lewis - Athletes as Educators
Twitter: @AngieL_GAMeN
Instagram: AngieL_GAMeN

Made in the USA
Charleston, SC
03 October 2016